MAKER LITERACIES
FOR ACADEMIC LIBRARIES

ALA Editions purchases fund advocacy, awareness, and accreditation programs for library professionals worldwide.

MAKER
LITERACIES
FOR ACADEMIC LIBRARIES

INTEGRATION INTO CURRICULUM

EDITED BY KATIE MUSICK PEERY

ALA Editions

CHICAGO | 2021

KATIE MUSICK PEERY is the director of the UTA FabLab at the University of Texas at Arlington Libraries. She provides leadership related to the development, management, and continuous improvement of the lab. Katie has published on diversifying makerspace student hiring and best practices for makerspace training to increase the inclusivity, impact, and efficacy of makerspaces on a college campus. Her grant work and research are primarily focused on integrating maker literacies into higher education curricula.

© 2021 by Katie Musick Peery

Extensive effort has gone into ensuring the reliability of the information in this book; however, the publisher makes no warranty, express or implied, with respect to the material contained herein.

ISBNs
978-0-8389-4806-4 (paper)
978-0-8389-4984-9 (PDF)
978-0-8389-4986-3 (ePub)
978-0-8389-4985-6 (Kindle)

Library of Congress Cataloging-in-Publication Data
Names: Peery, Katie Musick, 1988- editor.
Title: Maker literacies for academic libraries : integration into curriculum / edited by Katie Musick Peery.
Description: Chicago : ALA Editions, 2021. | Includes bibliographical references and index. | Summary: "This book inspires, empowers, and teaches librarians, makerspace staff, and faculty how to integrate their institution's makerspace into curriculum"— Provided by publisher.
Identifiers: LCCN 2020019596 | ISBN 9780838948064 (paper) | ISBN 9780838949863 (ebook) | ISBN 9780838949849 (pdf) | ISBN 9780838949856 (kindle)
Subjects: LCSH: Makerspaces in libraries—United States. | Maker movement in education—United States. | Academic libraries—Relations with faculty and curriculum—United States.
Classification: LCC Z716.37 .M34 2021 | DDC 025.5—dc23
LC record available at https://lccn.loc.gov/2020019596

Cover design by Kim Thornton. Text design by Alejandra Diaz in the Kepler Std, Filson Soft and Protipo typefaces.

♾ This paper meets the requirements of ANSI/NISO Z39.48-1992 (Permanence of Paper).

Printed in the United States of America
25 24 23 22 21   5 4 3 2 1

CONTENTS

PREFACE

As makerspaces become increasingly ubiquitous, many librarians have questioned the value these technologies bring to the library setting—is this just a fad to entice new users, or does engaging with these tools offer a true educational advantage? Even those librarians who believe in the benefits of makerspaces often then wonder, "What role could I possibly have in contributing to the success of such a space?"

Throughout the initial ideation, creation, and expansion of the Maker Literacies program, the University of Texas at Arlington (UTA) Libraries and FabLab staff consistently encountered these same questions, both for themselves and among makerspace staff at other university libraries. From the outset, we wanted to quantify the impact that academic library makerspaces were having on student learning, underscoring the anecdotal success stories we all hear with data which justified the programs and spaces that so many have worked to create. How best to accomplish that goal, as well as how best to share and encourage the adoption of such practices at other institutions, has been as experimental as any project that is created within the makerspace itself.

We set about our task by first drafting a rough set of maker-based competencies—transferable skills we believed students were gleaning by designing, fabricating, failing, and iterating in our collaborative, non–discipline-specific space. Internally, several faculty members partnered with us to pair selected competencies with their courses' learning outcomes, which we then assessed through pre- and post-assessments and faculty feedback. Although course integration of makerspaces occurs at many institutions, those programs often exist outside the library, are discipline-specific, or do not focus on assessment of the learning taking place. As this program evolved, we also wanted to specifically highlight the significant role librarians play in bridging the gap between the subject-based content students acquire in their courses and the interdisciplinary knowledge they can gain through making.

Thanks to external funding from the Institute of Museum and Library Services (IMLS), we have been able to continue to test and grow this program at other diverse institutions across the nation. More information about the origins of this program, accounts by all our partner institutions from the initial IMLS grant—Boise State University; the University of Massachusetts Amherst (UMass Amherst); the University of Nevada, Reno (UNR); and the University of North Carolina at Chapel Hill (UNC-Chapel Hill)—and the perspective of a faculty member are included within this book.

Through this work we have discovered that many librarians and makerspace staff members desire to establish a program like Maker Literacies at their institutions but are underprepared to partner with faculty in the curriculum development process; teaching and instructional design skills are often not emphasized in the traditional library school program, putting librarians at a disadvantage when working with faculty members who are also subject matter experts in their field. In other cases, space, staffing, or material constraints, or a lack of administrative support, impede progress or limit how courses can operate within a space.

Maker Literacies for Academic Libraries: Integration into Curriculum is written to inspire, encourage, educate, and empower librarians, makerspace staff, and faculty who are interested in integrating their makerspace into curriculum but have encountered difficulties such as those just noted or just aren't sure how to get started. The accounts within this book are presented by libraries serving a wide variety of user demographics, partnering with courses from a range of subjects, and all offering disparate equipment selections—no two are exactly alike, and each encountered its own unique challenges and successes in bringing this program to reality.

Collectively, UTA and our four partner academic library makerspaces from the first IMLS grant project have successfully refined and expanded the list of maker competencies to inclusively cover the broad scope of transferable skills that students obtain through maker-based course assignments. As a continuation of that work, UTA, UNR, and UMass Amherst are now partnered with seven other institutions, including UNC-Chapel Hill, to revise and improve standardized rubrics for each of those competencies to better assess student learning outcomes. We will also develop and host an immersion program for academic librarians and makerspace staff to impart best practices learned through this grant work, allowing participants to become curriculum design and assessment leaders within their local spheres of influence.

The future outcomes of the Maker Literacies team will continue to be shared broadly and openly for others to adopt and adapt. The assessment tools, immersion curricula, and analyses of student learning data will join the lesson plans and other resources currently found on the Maker Literacies website (library.uta.edu/makerliteracies) as they are developed and finalized. Our hope is that this book, along with these resources, will serve as an enduring, evolving, and impactful resource for librarians engaging in the maker movement for years to come!

—KATIE MUSICK PEERY

ACKNOWLEDGMENTS

The expansion and continued growth of the Maker Literacies program has been funded in part by two Institute of Museum and Library Services (IMLS) National Leadership Grants for Libraries.

The Maker Competencies and the Undergraduate Curriculum pilot program (LG-97-17-0010-17) enabled UTA Libraries to partner with four additional universities to test and improve our early-stage set of maker-based competencies and to develop best practices for integrating academic library makerspaces into the undergraduate curriculum.

Maker Immersion: Developing Curriculum Design and Assessment Skills for Academic Makerspace Course Integration (LG-17-19-0126-19), currently under way, will allow us to further broaden our impact and advance national practice through the development of rubrics for assessing student learning outcomes and the creation of a Maker Immersion program to elevate the professional development of librarians, makerspace staff, and faculty engaged in maker curriculum development.

Special thanks to all the library staff, makerspace staff, faculty members, and students who have participated in and given invaluable feedback for the growth of this program.

Teaching and Learning through Making

Gretchen Trkay and Rebecca Bichel

At the turn of the millennium, many people were pondering the future of academic libraries. *Library as place* had become a catchphrase as learning commons became ubiquitous in university libraries, but was there a future for libraries as providers of individual work and collaborative spaces? Some thinkers in the profession saw special collections and archives as the future of academic libraries, claiming that a library's value rested in its unique holdings and the access it created to that content. And a few of us had begun to consider the opportunities presented by the freedom of not being anchored to the role of collection caregiver. Could we become entrepreneurs, with our product being services and programming that strengthen students' expertise in and confidence with using cutting-edge tools to create and problem solve? The FabLab at the University of Texas at Arlington (UTA) Libraries represents one outcome of such a venture.

This chapter will explore, from two different perspectives, how UTA Libraries became a hub for making and maker-based education over the past six years. Specifically, Rebecca Bichel, the dean of UTA Libraries, will discuss the inception of our unique take on a makerspace and the intended goals at its creation, and Gretchen Trkay, our department head for Experiential Learning and Outreach, will explain how we approached actualizing a strategy for integrating making into curricula.

INSPIRATION AND INNOVATION IN LIBRARIES

BY REBECCA BICHEL

In 2012 UTA Libraries began an almost wholesale rethinking of what a library can be and, more specifically, what our library should be. Inspired by library thought leaders urging the profession to be bold, we began with a comprehensive data dive to uncover hidden needs and opportunities. We looked to qualitative and quantitative data that reflected university growth, enrollment, and library use but made certain to couple this research with bold ideas as well as best practices.

In the past decade, makerspaces in libraries have moved from exceptional to expected. Visionary Lauren Smedley created the first makerspace in a library in the United States at Fayetteville Free Library in New York State in spring 2011. In summer 2012, as UTA Libraries began planning for a pilot makerspace on the first floor of its Central Library, the DeLaMare Science and Engineering Library at the University of Nevada, Reno became the first academic library in the United States to make the leap to offering 3D services, including printing and scanning, to all students. Tod Colegrove, then director of the DeLaMare Library, noted that the maker service "takes the library's support of the learning and research missions of the University to a new level—beyond simple information exchange and consumption into knowledge-driven creation."[1]

A visitor to these makerspaces would find as much unique as shared, but what resonated most powerfully with me was a bold vision for technology as a tool to enable library users to move from consumers to creators. Dr. David Lankes, whose scholarship focuses on new librarianship, gave a revolutionary speech in October 2011 inciting librarians to act—to look to the future and not the past. His stated task was to "radicalize librarians." Lankes demanded we throw away the notion that we are in the "book business" in favor of the more noble goal of facilitating the creation of knowledge.[2] This vision inspired UTA Libraries to advantage neither the present nor the past in our thinking about how to empower our students to create.

This call for action was echoed by library influencer Brian Mathews in his 2012 white paper exhorting librarians to abandon a fixation on incremental enhancements to existing services, which he labeled as the quest for ever "better vacuum cleaners," in favor of bold ideas, transformative change, and attention to the user's real needs.[3] He noted, "Our jobs are shifting from doing what we've always done very well, to always being on the lookout for new opportunities to advance teaching, learning, service, and research." This perception resonated with UTA Libraries as we sought to integrate ourselves broadly in the university's ambitious new strategic plan rather than identify with a library-only mission. Both the university's and the Libraries' strategic plans prioritized enabling students as creators. From that strategic-level priority, a series of actions were planned, beginning with the creation of a cross-disciplinary makerspace, to be called the UTA FabLab, and retooling our instructional programs toward hands-on learning.

Creation of the FabLab

The UTA FabLab opened in 2014 and was the first MIT-affiliated FabLab in a university in Texas. The vision was that graduates with experience in the UTA FabLab would have a competitive advantage in the marketplace through their development of a rich toolkit of professional, creative, and technological skills.

In developing the UTA FabLab, we visited about thirty makerspaces across the country, some in libraries, but most not. Some on college campuses, some membership-based, and some open to the community. Our focus was not on what technology or tools to include but on best practices in developing a customer base, sustainability models, and the service model for each space.

A common phenomenon we saw in academic libraries was makerspaces housed in rooms with minimal hours and little, if any, dedicated staffing. These spaces sometimes seemed to exist more for the function of checking off an "Innovative Spaces in Libraries" bucket list item than for serving local needs. In addition, we saw many examples of the mini-me phenomenon—a space that was a mimicry of another makerspace or based on a published how-to list with no local conversation or data gathering.

We also saw incredible makerspaces. Some of our favorites were a makerspace in a public school in which the students had real ownership and there was a vision for equipping the students with life skills; a makerspace in a public library staffed entirely by volunteers but filled with locally grown innovations for local needs (e.g., using a digital studio to host indie music recordings); and a community makerspace in a socioeconomically depressed neighborhood that humbled us with how much the organizers accomplished with scraps and donations.

From these visits we fundamentally learned that if we wanted to build an indispensable makerspace and programming, we needed to be authentic to our students' needs and closely aligned with the core values and goals of our university and libraries. Although we have heard from other libraries about underused makerspaces, that was never the case at UTA. From its soft opening in 2014 as an eight-hundred-square-foot beta space through its expansion into an eight-thousand-square-foot facility, the UTA makerspace has been well used. I believe that this success came as a result of a series of carefully crafted decisions during the planning phases and continued responsiveness to the observed needs of our community.[4]

FabLab Design Strategies

The UTA FabLab space and programming were designed with specific goals that drove decision-making. For example, we wanted to attract a broad cross section of students, rather than a specific discipline or class level. So we strategically located the FabLab on the first floor of our Central Library, highly visible as soon as you enter, and not in a specialized library. We wanted students to feel welcomed, so the space is adjacent to our café, is completely open to the library (no walls), and has a mix of study tables and worktables. We wanted diverse students across disciplines to use the space, so we made a policy decision to aggressively recruit student employees across disciplines, gender identities, and ages, recognizing that this diversity requires a resource investment in building the technical skills of many student employees. Absent this policy, we would likely be staffed almost entirely by male engineering students.

The following strategic decisions governed design:

1. *The development of the UTA FabLab was one outcome of a broad strategic goal related to creation.* The FabLab was never a one-off or just a space. It was developed as a distinct public services department with associated staffing and services. The department was later partnered with

another new department, now called Experiential Learning and Outreach, responsible for developing course-integrated and independent learning opportunities grounded in a philosophy of experiential learning (discussed later in this chapter).

2. *The UTA FabLab would be available for any student.*

No class-only limits. Because there was a shortage of learning labs, we heard strong faculty advocacy that the FabLab be limited to classes only and curricular use, excluding walk-in students or recreational projects. We instead advocated to stakeholders the value of a makerspace open to all students across majors. We want students in the makerspace anytime, exploring and applying their creativity. We design pop-up programming to encourage this aspect.

No limits to majors or class levels. Because there was a shortage at UTA of labs in which engineering and architecture students could work, initially there was an external expectation that those majors would be our target audience. Instead, we aggressively market to all colleges. Knowing that student employees bring their friends and classmates to visit the FabLab, our goal is to have student employees from each college on campus in our long semesters. We also promote the space as STEAHM (Science, Technology, Engineering, Arts, Humanities, and Math), not STEM.

Value and work for diversity. Because UTA is one of the most diverse universities in the country, we knew we wanted to help overcome the inherent barriers of a perceived STEM space to non-STEM majors and women.[5] Our recruitment strategy for student employees reflects this goal. We recruit faculty across disciplines to engage with their students in the FabLab. This outreach has included disabilities studies, English, art, math, education, modern languages, engineering, architecture, biology, philosophy, theater, broadcast communication, and history. I am proud that though leadership for discipline-specific fabrication labs is overwhelmingly male, our director is a woman and a librarian.[6] This key position sets the tone for our commitment to diversity.

3. *Embrace risk-taking and play.* Much of the equipment is not heavily mediated. Rules are limited, such as those for safety. Like the rest of the library,

we want the students to feel ownership of the FabLab. They are *not* our guests. This is their home. That means they have spaces to relax, explore, and experiment. Skilled technicians and student employees help students craft solutions for complex class assignments as well as make fantastical figures for tabletop games. At the same time, although mentors are available, we celebrate failure as an inherent, valuable learning experience. Another way we enable risk-taking and play is by subsidizing costs significantly. Students pay for the consumables we provide (comparable to paying to print or photocopy) but not for use of the equipment.

4. *Build a full-time staff with technical expertise.* Most library makerspaces are staffed by student employees or volunteers or one staff member, often with other assignments. The UTA FabLab has five full-time staff in addition to our student employees. The two technicians were recruited for their deep technical expertise, and an artist with an advanced degree (MFA), experience creating with maker technologies, and curriculum development and teaching experience but without an MLS was hired as a FabLab librarian. The Libraries received zero new positions for the FabLab, so we repurposed empty lines from other roles.

5. *Minimize barriers to access.* We want students to see the FabLab immediately upon entering the Central Library and to feel welcomed to enter and explore. The space has a casual, industrial design—cement floors, tables hand-crafted from pipe and wood, and colorful balls with retractable electrical cords suspended from the ceiling. There are no walls enclosing the space other than clear glass doors to contain the shop room, and study tables and computer-use tables are purposely integrated to encourage a mix of uses. The space includes a large sectional and other soft seating, as well as oversized bar-height tables. We selected a furniture style inspired by community co-working spaces to encourage collaboration and entrepreneurship. The UTA FabLab is adjacent to our café, and food and drink are welcome anywhere in the makerspace, with the exception of our shop room where they would pose a safety risk.

The goal for UTA was never simply to build a makerspace. We knew we needed to build a dynamic space to support our strategic goal of supporting creation, but we also needed paired services, programming, and outreach that integrated making within the curriculum as one of the university strategies to enhance student academic and professional success.

The UTA FabLab is unique as a library makerspace because it was conceptualized as an integrated space with a broad vision of what a modern, twenty-first-century research library should be. We made a decision to offer campus leadership focused on student creativity, innovation, and entrepreneurship; developed a strategy to advance that leadership goal; and created a makerspace as one element of that mission. Our next step was to redesign our instructional program to draw upon the tools and expertise offered via the FabLab to transform our teaching from active to experiential learning.

INNOVATION IN TEACHING AND LEARNING PRACTICE

BY GRETCHEN TRKAY

In direct response to our strategic imperative to be a hub for experiential learning and creation, the Libraries built the UTA FabLab, a space in which students could engage in both self-directed and guided inquiry and creation. This strategic imperative promised the UTA community access to "a transformative environment that fosters learning through reflection, design, creativity, experimentation, and innovation."[7] The FabLab provided that space and service model, and students quickly began to engage in self-directed learning, but we struggled to identify a sustainable strategy for curricular integration and programming. Although FabLab staff worked with faculty to devise new course assignments, the original strategy to partner in this work with the Libraries' subject liaisons failed.

In 2013 UTA Libraries initiated a comprehensive reorganization. Until that point, subject librarians had been asked to do what subject librarians had always done—consult with students and faculty, provide bibliographic instruction, give input about collections, and occasionally work the reference desk. The new vision included the creation of an outreach and scholarship department. Members of this department would continue to have responsibility for traditional subject librarian activities but would add new layers of expertise, with an emphasis on scholarly communication and hands-on learning.

As is not uncommon in a perpetual beta environment, sometimes you try things and they just don't work. Our library staff had a mixed reaction to focusing on creation as a primary library function. A few staff members were excited about the makerspace and became early evangelists. Some were open but concerned about sustainability with limited resources and how staff would develop technical skills. And some rejected the concept of a library role beyond information access and preservation. Many of our subject librarians were overwhelmed with the substantive shift in what they were being asked to achieve.

The reality of working within the context of a makerspace is that it requires a set of competencies different from what many librarians have been trained to do.[8] Rather than emphasizing mastery of academic subjects, information retrieval, and evaluation, those librarians engaged in makerspaces require dispositions that embrace collaboration, adaptability, and learning on the fly, along with such hard skills as program development, grant writing, technology literacy, and a deep grounding in the application of learning theory. The Libraries had not effectively laid the foundation for all our liaison librarians to engage in this new type of librarianship. The closest correlation to the dispositions and skills just listed was found in our librarians who had been heavily involved in teaching and learning and in undergraduate student engagement activities. One of these librarians, who had been initially hired as a first-year-experience librarian and then transitioned into a position as an interim codirector for the FabLab (and who also happens to be the editor of this book), was hired as the full-time director of the FabLab. Within a year of that hire, I, a former information literacy librarian, was tasked with creating a new department for which integrating making into curricula would be among its primary responsibilities. My approach to accomplishing this task was to take what I knew and find a way to apply this knowledge and experience in support of empowering students as creators.

Experiential Learning as a Pedagogical Frame

Experiential learning is an educational model predicated on students learning by reflecting on doing.[9] The experiential education ecosystem includes high-impact practices such as project-based learning, problem-based learning, service learning, undergraduate research, and study abroad.[10] Experiential curricula make it possible for students to pair and apply subject-based learning with transferable skills. Essential to these curricula are reflective exercises during which students are encouraged to synthesize their experiences with

FIGURE 1.1

Kolb's experiential learning cycle

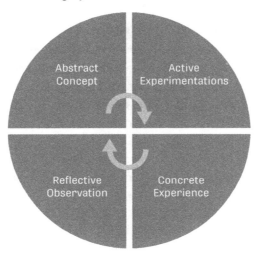

Source: Derived from David A. Kolb, *Experiential Learning: Experience as the Source of Learning and Development* (Englewood Cliffs, NJ: Prentice-Hall, 1984).

prior knowledge, draw conclusions from the experience, and connect new knowledge with potential future applications (figure 1.1).

Our new department, Experiential Learning and Undergraduate Research (later changed to Experiential Learning and Outreach), embraced experiential learning as its preferred mode for teaching and learning because that model is student-centered and student-specific. Grounded in students' experiences and their individualized reflection, experiential learning allows for those with differing initial knowledge bases to achieve similar growth trajectories, even if they do not ultimately land in the same place. The reflective nature of experiential learning also makes room for the inclusion of instructional strategies that support transferability. Kuglitsch illustrates this feature in her discussion of low and high road transfer within the context of information literacy.[11] Specifically, library educators can develop instruction during which students start by exploring a technique or idea (active experimentation and concrete experience) followed by connecting this exploration to other concepts and contexts (reflection and abstract conception), techniques Kuglitsch refers to as "hugging" and "bridging."

Maker-Based Competencies

Experiential learning is broader than making alone, but the first goal for the Experiential Learning and Undergraduate Research Department was to develop structure and programming for curricular integration of making and low barrier to entry opportunities for guided exploration. Creating a concept for how the department would hire and train librarians and staff, engage with faculty, collaborate with our partners in the Libraries' FabLab, and develop curricula that bridge subject-based learning and transferable skills was our first task. The most profound experience that I had as a librarian was attending the Information Literacy Immersion program presented in 2005 by the Association of College and Research Libraries (ACRL) and the subsequent application of what I had learned to my teaching and learning practice. I had successfully fostered collaborations with faculty by using the ACRL's *Information Literacy Competency Standards for Higher Education* as a tool for mapping what the Libraries could provide to faculty members' goals for students' disciplinary learning. Just as information and digital literacies bolster libraries' position as a hub for teaching transferable and transdisciplinary skills, my thought was that by defining maker literacy as a concept, the Libraries would be able to more easily talk to faculty about the applicability of making outside STEAM disciplines. I made the decision that the Libraries would develop competencies that helped define the transferable skills students could gain via making. Before we even began trying this approach as a strategy, I had dreams of creating a national immersion program that would provide librarians engaged with making what information literacy immersion had provided me.

Simultaneous with this decision, ACRL approved the *Framework for Information Literacy for Higher Education,* an effective argument that information literacy, rather than being a set of transdisciplinary skills, had theoretical significance outside disciplinary contexts. This shift in how academic libraries were thinking about information literacy gave me pause about whether maker-based competencies were the right approach to creating structure for our work with faculty. It is fair to argue that reliance on competencies to define concepts such as design thinking, information literacy, and the like can be perceived as reductionist, but what the Libraries needed was a bridge for conversation and collaboration with subject faculty that resulted in incorporating the learning of complex, maker-based transferable skills into subject-based curricula. When thinking about the integration of making into courses, I felt that we needed to reflect on something concrete, something not unlike Kolb's experiential learning cycle (see figure 1.1), before we would be in a place to articulate an abstract concept of making equivalent to ACRL's *Framework*.

An additional consideration was whether pursuing goals that resulted in assessment of student learning in makerspaces was antithetical to fostering a home for maker culture. Many argue that makerspaces should only be used for informal learning and that by applying structures of formal academic environments, student learning will be stymied. It is a fair critique. Our position was that guided, course-integrated making with measurement of student learning was only one of a multitude of ways in which students could engage with iterative design and creation. Additionally, if course assignments, activities, and instruction are carefully structured, there is still room for students to explore, invent, and problem solve as part of their process. Ultimately, we felt that for libraries to be able to meet the expectations of university administrations, we needed to show return on investment through usage statistics and tangible evidence of student learning.

Getting the Work Done

With a path forward in mind, we needed to determine how best to staff a department that would not work specifically for the makerspace but for which one of the primary responsibilities would be integrating making into courses. Due to the nature of our library, our first hire would also be responsible for traditional subject liaison duties. Our strategy was to hire a librarian who was trained in a discipline that would easily pair with design thinking and creation and who demonstrated excitement about the opportunity to develop some foundational competencies and tools for curricular integration of making. Martin Wallace was hired as UTA Libraries' new Maker Literacies librarian and liaison to the College of Engineering. His first task was to pull together a team of subject faculty and FabLab staff to create a beta set of maker competencies that we could use to test course integration and assessment of learning on a local level. This endeavor will be discussed in greater detail in the next chapter, but the team's expected outcome was the development and testing of the competencies so that we would be prepared to apply for a planning grant from the Institute of Museum and Library Services (IMLS)

National Leadership Grants for Libraries program that would fund testing of the competencies at different college and university library makerspaces throughout the country. UTA Libraries was awarded this grant in 2017, and we continue to work with partners nationally to refine and build on our initial work to integrate making into academic coursework.

THE PRESENT AND FUTURE

BY REBECCA BICHEL AND GRETCHEN TRKAY

UTA Libraries' Experiential Learning and Outreach Department continues to expand its work. The trajectory of our work includes curricular integration of both fabrication and digital-based making, pop-up experiential learning opportunities intended for beginning makers, maker-based curriculum and professional development for K–12 audiences, and the development of virtual reality health sciences educational platforms. In partnership with the FabLab, UMass Amherst, and UNR, we received a 2019 IMLS National Leadership Grants for Libraries project grant (LG-17-19-0126-19) to create a national networking and professional development immersion program intended to prepare other librarians to integrate making in courses and assess student learning. Specifically, this grant will fund the development and testing of rubrics for each of the maker literacy competencies discussed in this book. Faculty, librarians, and makerspace staff will be able to apply these rubrics to student artifacts as a direct assessment of student learning and development of maker-based skills. Additionally, the IMLS National Leadership project grant will fund the creation of an immersion program for librarians and library makerspace staff at other institutions. This program will be offered both in person and through an asynchronous, digital platform. All lesson plans, assessments, and course materials created as part of both IMLS grants are available with Creative Commons licenses for reuse and adaptation by others (library.uta.edu/makerliteracies). Our intent is to create an ever-growing repository of curricula as a resource for educators worldwide.

UTA Libraries continues to expand its support for its ultimate goal: to empower students as creators through teaching and learning. The FabLab, the Experiential Learning and Undergraduate Research Department, and the Maker Literacies program were the first expressions of this goal, but the future includes a plan to expand the space available for students to engage in creative activities. The concept is to dedicate the entire first floor of our Central Library to creativity across disciplines. Students will be able to develop mastery using cutting-edge technologies, adding robust digital creation technologies to the fabrication tools currently available in the FabLab. Our vision is to provide an immersive, technology-rich environment in which students, including K–12 students in nearby schools, can engage as creators, facilitated by librarians and staff committed to experiential learning.

NOTES

1. "DeLaMare Science and Engineering Library First in Nation to Offer 3D Printing Campuswide," *Nevada Today,* July 19, 2012, https://www.unr.edu/nevada-today/news/2012/3d-copier.

2. R. David Lankes, "Killing Librarianship" (keynote speech, New England Library Association, Burlington, VT, October 2, 2011), https://davidlankes.org/rdlankes/Presentations/2011/KillLib.htm.

3. Brian Mathews, "Think Like a Startup: A White Paper to Inspire Library Entrepreneurialism" (2012), https://vtechworks.lib.vt.edu/handle/10919/18649.

4. Katie Musick Peery and Morgan Chivers, "Intentionally Cultivating Diverse Community for Radically Open Access Makerspaces" (white paper, International Symposium on Academic Makerspaces, Stanford, CA, 2018), http://hdl.handle.net/10106/27574.

5. "Campus Ethnic Diversity: National Universities," *U.S. News and World Report* (2019), https://www.usnews.com/best-colleges/rankings/national-universities/campus-ethnic-diversity.

6. Youngmoo E. Kim, Kareem Edouard, Katelyn Alderfer, and Brian K. Smith, *Making Culture: A National Study of Education Makerspaces* (Drexel University, ExCITe Center, 2018), https://drexel.edu/excite/engagement/learning-innovation/making-culture-report.

7. *Plunging Forward: The University of Texas at Arlington Libraries 2020 Strategic Plan,* https://rc.library.uta.edu/uta-ir/handle/10106/25818.

8. Kyungwon Koh and June Abbas, "Competencies for Information Professionals in Learning Labs and Makerspaces," *Journal of Education for Library and Information Science* 56, no. 2 (2015): 114–29, doi:10.12783/issn.2328-2967/56/2/3.

9. David A. Kolb, *Experiential Learning: Experience as the Source of Learning and Development* (Englewood Cliffs, NJ: Prentice-Hall, 1984).

10. Jay W. Roberts, *Experiential Education in the College Context: What It Is, How It Works, and Why It Matters* (New York, NY: Routledge, 2016).

11. Rebecca Kuglitsch, "Teaching for Transfer: Reconciling the Framework with Disciplinary Information Literacy," *portal: Libraries and the Academy* 15, no. 3 (July 2015): 457–70.

Who, What, and Why
Contextualizing Maker Literacies for Academic Libraries

Martin K. Wallace

n 2016, in collaboration with the University of Texas at Arlington (UTA) Libraries' FabLab and faculty representing a wide range of academic units at UTA, I began piloting UTA Libraries' Maker Literacies program, tying maker-based competencies to the learning objectives of undergraduate courses and assisting faculty members with makerspace curriculum design. The goals of the program are to equip undergraduate students from all disciplines with transferable, cross-disciplinary skills (for example, teamwork and collaboration, project management, and technical communication) gained from hands-on, project-based learning in makerspaces and to familiarize students with technology that will become ever more ubiquitous across all industries and disciplines. We seek to include courses from all programs of study, including the humanities, social sciences, and fine arts, as well as traditional STEM fields.

This chapter is written especially for librarians, library administrators, and other staff who have doubts about the library's role in makerspaces and maker literacies programs. This chapter will highlight several takeaways from the early phases of this program, experiences that helped me reconcile with my own new role as the Maker Literacies librarian. I will define maker competencies and provide contextualization for academic libraries regarding why we are uniquely situated to be leaders in the realm of makerspaces and makerspace literacy. I will discuss the history of the program and development of the list of maker competencies and explain how that early work prepared us for an Institute of Museum and Library Services (IMLS) planning grant that garnered national recognition. I will describe some courses that have gone through the program and explain how to get your courses involved. By the end of this chapter, I hope to have guided you through my transformation from a mindset of "curious while skeptical" to a mindset of "true believer," and I hope that many of you will join me in that transformation.

MAKER COMPETENCIES DEFINED

As the label implies, maker competencies are the skills, talents, and dispositions that one acquires or improves upon while problem solving and working on projects in makerspaces or similar learning environments. However, although learners can develop any number of technology-specific competencies while working in makerspaces—depending on the types of technology made available within the specific makerspace—we intentionally focus the scope to higher-level, technology-agnostic, cross-disciplinary, transferable competencies that one may acquire or strengthen when working in makerspaces. A quick review of our lists of maker competencies (appendixes A and B) reveals no mention of 3D printers, Arduino products, or any of the other popular technologies commonly found in makerspaces today; what one will find are competencies related to collaboration, communication, critical thinking, design thinking, and project management. Although the competencies are not dependent on specific equipment or technology, we do still look for competence attainment in students' use of whichever tools they choose or are assigned to use. The maker competencies are, by design, universal in their application across disciplines and industries, highly sought after by employers, and often referred to as 21st Century Competencies, soft skills, or otherwise technology-independent aptitudes.

CONTEXTUALIZING FOR ACADEMIC LIBRARIES

The concept of Maker Literacies first came to my attention shortly after I began my new position at UTA Libraries, an event that just happened to occur right on the heels of a major library reorganization. All I knew up to this point was that I would be the Libraries' liaison to the College of Engineering and that my job would have "something to do with" UTA Libraries' FabLab (UTA's academic library makerspace). My new department would now be known as Experiential Learning and Undergraduate Research. More important, we were assigned our new leadership roles and charges, mine being the Maker Literacies librarian, to spearhead the creation of a Maker Literacies program (perhaps the world's first) that would integrate an academic library makerspace into the under-graduate curriculum through collaborative curriculum development and assessment. At that time, there were certainly other campus makerspaces in which students worked on assigned projects, but ours would be the first (to the best of my knowledge) to structure a program from the ground up, based on pedagogically tested curriculum design methodology, with a primary goal of measuring its impact on student learning in a meaningful way.

Now that I had my fancy new title and intriguing new charge, I had to stop and ask myself, "Who are we, as librarians, to create this thing called *Maker Literacies*—especially myself as an admitted outsider to the actual maker movement?" A significant portion of the work ahead would be to figure out what competencies learners acquire in makerspaces and outline some competency standards for measuring that learning. If the maker community wants competency standards for measuring learning, shouldn't the members of that community be the ones to articulate those standards? Think about it—it was the larger library community that drafted the ACRL's *Information Literacy Competency Standards for Higher Education.* What might those stan-dards have looked like if left to any other profession to compile on our behalf?

On the other hand, my experience and qualifications made me an ideal person for this type of work. I have been an engineering liaison librarian for the past fourteen years. I hold a BFA in sculpture, have used many of the tools found in makerspaces, and understand the creative process. I hold an MS in information systems engineering, for which I gained a solid grasp of the engineering design life cycle. As a former patents and trademarks librarian, I have worked with inventors, entrepreneurs, and innovators and have spe-cialized in intellectual property issues relevant to creators. Having previously designed and taught information literacy and patent searching courses online and in the classroom, I have a sound understanding of curriculum design, instruction, and assessment. Last, I share the maker ethos of experimentation, sharing, and collaboration. All these attributes qualified me perfectly for the job I was about to undertake. Fears, doubts, and anxieties all set aside, I knew that if any librarian was going to do this work, it might as well be me.

MY TRANSFORMATION FROM NAYSAYER TO POLLYANNA

In July 2016 I had the opportunity to present my team's fledgling work at the one-day-long TX STEM Librarians Conference (now known as STEM Librarians South) at Texas Tech University. This was mere months after taking on my new role as Maker Literacies librarian and forming the task force that would collaboratively develop the Maker Literacies pilot program. At this point, all we had was a plan and an early draft of the list of competencies, but no other deliverables. I was prepared to talk about the formation of the task force, our mission and goals, and our plans for a fall 2016 pilot test of the program. My presentation would be the last session of the day, and I had a sense of dread about introducing my work to a room full of librarians who were probably tired, cognitively overloaded, or worse—not interested in a session topic foreign or irrelevant to their own work. I felt that most of the audience would bail before I got my time in the spotlight. Several attendees had already admitted that they would be leaving early to catch flights. My morale was low, and anxiety high.

Fortunately, thanks to the keynote address that morning, my dread melted into eager anticipation. Dr. Dominick Casadonte, the Minnie Stevens Piper Professor in the Department of Chemistry and Biochemistry at Texas Tech University, delivered an impassioned and convincing plea for libraries and librarians to rise to the emerging (and admittedly ambiguous) needs of today's STEAM (Science, Technology, Engineering, Art, and Mathematics) educators. In one and a half hours, he breezed through the history of the arts and sciences, beginning with Aristotle. He discussed the "siloization" of academia, explaining how the arts and sciences became ever more isolated from one another, separating into increasingly granular silos of knowledge. For example, said Casadonte, "we're living in a time where biochemists and molecular biologists don't read the same scholarly journals, don't attend the same conferences, and don't know how to communicate with one another." His argument was that if biochemists and molecular biologists can't communicate, we can't expect a biologist to be able to effectively communicate with an artist, an engineer, or a business manager, because the roots of their education have taken them all in such divergent directions.

The genesis of the concept of "STEM" can be found in the National Science Foundation's 1990 response to the siloing of academia. Although the intent of the foundation's initiative was to break down barriers in academia, educators and practitioners were recalcitrant and unable to adapt to the interdisciplinary, multidisciplinary, and transdisciplinary requirements of true STEM-based teaching. It took a years-long cultural shift in our ways of thinking to undo our old habits, and only now are we beginning to see the potential for a truly STEM-based curriculum in academia.

STEM-based curriculum is an attempt to bring the sciences, technology, engineering, and mathematics back under one umbrella, where curriculum is problem-based and learning outcomes hinge on the student being able to incorporate aspects of all four disciplines into one holistic understanding of the world. It is a good step in the right direction, but Casadonte argued that the STEM approach doesn't take interdisciplinarity far enough. Adoption of STEAM (in which the *A* represents both the arts and the humanities, according to Casadonte) is the next step toward truly holistic education.

Revelatory to me was Casadonte's articulate emphasis on the use of "transdisciplinary" spaces, software, technology, services, and events. The word *transdisciplinary,* so I thought, was cobbled together from the concepts of "interdisciplinary" and "transferable" skills, a central and foundational principle baked into our Maker Literacies program; this was the first time I had seen or heard the word used any place else. To my great surprise, "transdisciplinarity" was already an established idea in academia, but one that I was completely unaware of. This marked a dramatic convergence in my mind, and now I was beginning to see the significance and relevance of my work with Maker Literacies in a broader context.

Casadonte defined *transdisciplinary* as (I paraphrase) "research conducted by investigators from different areas of study to jointly create new conceptual, theoretical, and methodological frameworks that integrate and move beyond discipline-specific approaches to address real-world problems."

Casadonte wrapped up his presentation with a specific list of what libraries need to support STEAM-based educators:

- Librarians who understand and are excited by the notion of STEAM
- STEM librarians (in single or multiple disciplines) who have experience with the A field in order to provide meaningful resources for the particular STEAM practitioner
- Transdisciplinary librarians
- Librarians who are familiar with interdisciplinary and transdisciplinary journals and literature
- Librarians who can help bridge the language gaps across STEAM areas of interest
- Librarians who are skilled in visualization literature and, if possible, software
- Librarians who are skilled in 3D analysis and makerspaces

Most obvious for our purposes is the last item in the list—"librarians who are skilled in 3D analysis and makerspaces"—but every item in the list rings true to what the Maker Literacies program has been after: a truly transdisciplinary educational makerspace experience for every undergraduate student at UTA, a project-based learning environment in which students can explore ideas from the arts, the humanities, business, engineering, writing, and more. As I listened to Casadonte's presentation, I kept hearing more themes that would overlap with my own presentation; in a fortunate and serendipitous stroke of luck, my presentation was going to provide the perfect bookend to Casadonte's keynote talk. Here we had an actual STEM professor proclaiming that STEM must reintegrate to some degree, that the arts and humanities must also reintegrate with all of STEM to some degree, and that libraries can help by providing transdisciplinary spaces, software, technology, services, and events. My presentation about the Maker Literacies program would show librarians attempting to do many of the things Casadonte recommended. It should go without saying that my dread and anxiety had vanished, replaced by excitement, and I couldn't wait to give my presentation!

To wrap up this anecdote, I'm happy to report that my presentation was well received and that I was not the only one who saw the overlap with the keynote speech. Although many attendees had left (including Dr. Casadonte, unfortunately), plenty remained and were surprisingly engaged; several stayed a half hour after the conference ended for additional conversation and Q&A about the Maker Literacies program. Although that in itself was great, I think the most important takeaway is that this little conference had such a huge impact on how I think about the role of academic libraries in the makerspace and maker literacies domains—academic libraries are uniquely situated to be key players in them. Academic libraries provide equitable and democratic access to resources, regardless of discipline. Our organizations are transdisciplinary by design, with expertise in nearly every subject area. Academic libraries have broad and deep connections with the rest of the campus, including subject faculty with whom we routinely collaborate on instruction. Most academic libraries are moving books into off-site storage in order to open up additional spaces for learning and creativity. Moreover, we are used to measuring things, recording statistics, and performing assessments of our programs. Combined, these characteristics scream for a library makerspace and for a way to assess the impact of the makerspace on student learning! The Maker Literacies program at UTA takes advantage of all these strengths to provide rich experiences for students related to making and to assess the impact of those experiences on learning outcomes.

THE MAKER LITERACIES TASK FORCE

I'm going to jump back in time, just a little, to describe the establishment of the aforementioned Maker Literacies Task Force. Once I had my charge to lead a team to create, implement, and assess a Maker Literacies program at UTA Libraries, the next step was to put together the task force. Nervous? Yes, I was! Suffering a little impostor syndrome? You bet! However, I was reassured by the facts that UTA's 2015–2017 Quality Enhancement Plan (QEP) theme was "Experiential Learning," so there was already awareness on campus about this topic, and that several faculty members from various departments were either inquiring about or already using the FabLab for their experiential course projects. Then–UTA president Vistasp Karbhari was behind the Libraries' initiatives 100 percent, and the culture of UTA, not least of its Libraries, encourages bold ideas for transforming education, taking risks, and bestowing reward rather than punishment for failure-in-earnest.

I have to admit that putting the task force together ended up being one of the easiest parts of the plan. Unlike my previous experiences with trying to push information literacy on uninterested subject faculty, I had a lineup of potential faculty who had already voiced their willingness to participate. All I had to do, for the most part, was ask. Three of us at the Libraries were de facto members of the budding task force: Morgan Chivers, FabLab technician and artist-in-residence; Katie Musick Peery, director of the UTA FabLab; and myself. Together we listed faculty members who had already used or shown interest in using the FabLab for their coursework, and others who had already expressed willingness to help create the program. Once I had my initial list of names, I used a snowball recruitment method, inviting each potential task force member by e-mail and asking each invitee to recommend other potential participants. Only a few invitees declined to participate, and before I knew it, I had an interdisciplinary task force:

Amanda Alexander (Art Education)
Estee Beck (English)
Bonnie Boardman (Engineering)
Morgan Chivers (UTA Libraries, FabLab)
Katie Musick Peery (UTA Libraries, FabLab)
Kathryn Pole (Education)
Jennifer Roye (Nursing)
David Sparks (Science Education)
Martin Wallace (UTA Libraries)

Because faculty buy-in was greater than expected, recruitment didn't take long at all. We were able to quickly get started on the work ahead of us. By May 2016 we already had our first draft list of maker competencies ready to test in several pilot courses, and by fall 2016 we had several courses ready to test them.

Having accomplished its three tasks of creating a list of maker competencies, identifying faculty and courses to test the competencies, and assessing the program, the Maker Literacies Task Force was discharged in August 2017. A Maker Literacies Program Team assumed the responsibilities for moving the program forward. This team consisted of Gretchen Trkay (department head, Experiential Learning and Outreach), Katie Musick Peery (director of the UTA FabLab), Morgan Chivers (now the FabLab librarian and artist-in-residence), and myself (Maker Literacies librarian). Since then, the Maker Literacies Program Team has been responsible for coordinating, assessing, growing, and continually improving the program.

DEVELOPMENT OF THE LIST OF MAKER COMPETENCIES

The first task of the newly formed Maker Literacies Task Force was to identify a set of transdisciplinary skills, talents, and dispositions that undergraduate students could acquire and improve upon while working on projects in makerspaces. We accomplished this task in three phases between March 2016 and December 2018. In March 2016 the Maker Literacies Task Force was formed. Task force members spent that first semester (spring 2016) gauging faculty interests, conducting an exhaustive literature review, attending Maker Faires and similar conferences, interviewing makers (teachers and learners alike) at Dallas-Fort Worth–area makerspaces, and directly observing those working in makerspaces.

A major influence on the development of the list of competencies was the National Association of Colleges and Employers (NACE) Job Outlook 2016. The Job Outlook reports findings from its survey of top companies that actively recruit recent college graduates. The report identifies the top attributes that employers look for in a college graduate's résumé, such as leadership, teamwork, communication, and problem-solving skills. The Maker Literacies team quickly realized that many of the attributes are skills that students can develop by working on projects in makerspaces. Developing these skills, theoretically, will make our graduates more competitive in the job market. The overwhelming majority of the attributes on the list are transdisciplinary by nature and benefit students from any major.

A second major influence on the development of the list of competencies was the ACRL's *Information Literacy Competency Standards for Higher Education*. After conducting our preliminary investigative work, we brainstormed a long list of potential student learning outcomes gleaned from our research, from the very broad to the very narrow. Next, we reviewed the list and grouped the outcomes into larger, more general "standards" and "performance indicators." The resulting outcomes reflected not only our own perceived notions of what students could learn in a makerspace but also the actual desirable outcomes that met specific course objectives as outlined within, or derived from, existing course syllabi. If this approach sounds familiar, that's because it is roughly the same process that the ACRL (on a much larger scale) implemented to create the *Information Literacy Competency Standards for Higher Education*. Because I had very little recent experience in making but a lot of recent experience with the ACRL Standards, it made a lot of sense to use that process as a springboard into developing the Maker Literacies program.

Beginning in fall 2016 and lasting through fall 2017, we pilot tested the draft list of competencies in thirteen unique courses at UTA, some with multiple sections and some repeating over multiple semesters. This testing was the second developmental phase for the list of competencies. The task force gathered feedback from participating faculty regarding the challenges of integrating the FabLab into their courses, usefulness of the list of maker competencies in planning their curriculum, and effectiveness of the Maker Literacies program, including evidence of student learning. We used feedback gathered from fall 2016 and spring 2017 participating faculty to refine the draft list of maker competencies during our first major assessment of the program in summer 2017. This version of the list we titled our beta list of maker competencies, and we began testing them in the third developmental phase, the IMLS-funded partnership phase, described in more detail later in this chapter.

During the IMLS-funded partnership phase, the grant team gathered additional feedback from librarians, makerspace staff, and faculty participants from UTA and our four partner sites, covering the same topics in the initial UTA-only pilot phase: the challenges of integrating makerspaces into courses, usefulness of the beta list of maker competencies in planning curriculum, and effectiveness of the Maker Literacies program. Participants from both phases provided a tremendous amount of actionable feedback about the usefulness of the beta-phase list of competencies, including recommendations for additions to the list. After a thorough review of all feedback, the grant team revised and publicly released its list of maker competencies in December 2018. The list of competencies (appendix B) is optimized for easy mapping to course learning outcomes, or the competencies can simply be copied and pasted into curricula as learning outcomes.

IMLS GRANT

Even in its earliest days, the task force endeavored to iterate the Maker Literacies program a few times before ultimately publishing our official, revised list of maker competencies. We were also eager to create a repository of case studies and sample curricula cocreated with participating faculty to share with the world. We knew that we couldn't do this without help from other academic library makerspaces because we wanted to present a program that had been tested in a variety of settings to ensure that it was adaptable for diverse audiences.

At about the time that we finished our first draft of the list of competencies, the Maker Literacies Program Team, joined by Dr. Kathryn Pole (assistant professor of literacy studies, serving as consultant), formed a grant writing team. Evelyn Barker, then UTA Libraries' director of grants and special projects, was a de facto member of the team. Evelyn provided grant writing support and pre- and post-award administrative assistance and served on all UTA Libraries' grant projects.

I also invited Tara Radniecki, engineering librarian at the University of Nevada, Reno (UNR) to serve on the grant writing team and to lead the Maker Literacies pilot at UNR if and when we were awarded a grant. I discovered Tara's work while conducting my initial literature review and landscape analysis of other institutions engaged in maker literacies work; coincidentally, Dean Rebecca Bichel and members of the FabLab team were also familiar with the UNR staff members and their innovative work with library makerspaces. Tara's work at UNR emphasized the need for libraries to steer their maker assets toward curricular integration, and she was also vocal about the need to measure the impacts of academic library makerspaces on student learning. Those two aspects set her work apart from other initiatives that I was able to find at the time. By the time I formed the grant writing group, I already knew I wanted her on the team.

In September 2016 the grant writing team submitted a preliminary two-page proposal for an IMLS National Leadership Grants for Libraries planning grant for the purposes of piloting the Maker Literacies program at additional academic library makerspaces, revising the list of competencies, and creating a repository of curricula. If awarded, this planning grant would incentivize up to three additional institutional partners, for a total of five (UNR was already a committed partner), at which to pilot test our early-stage Maker Literacies program. The grant would fund small stipends for teaching faculty at each partner institution, materials for pilot courses, and travel for members of the planning team to visit partner institutions.

In early December 2016 we received an invitation from IMLS to submit our full ten-page proposal. Fortunately, we were able to muscle through and deliver our proposal, "Maker Competencies and the Undergraduate Curriculum," by the mid-January deadline, and in April 2017 IMLS awarded the grant

(National Leadership Grants for Libraries LG-97-17-0010-17). At that time, we began the process of identifying potential program partners and then visiting the academic library makerspaces on our short list. To identify potential partners for the project, we used data gathered in a 2016 makerspace survey, reviewed current literature and the internet to find academic library maker-spaces doing similar work, and attended conferences at which we mined for leads. By July 2017 when the grant work officially kicked off, we had compiled a list of twenty-two academic library makerspaces that showed evidence of integrating their makerspace into coursework, strong librarian-faculty relations, and a culture of assessment. We ranked them according to various criteria using a scored partnership selection rubric and then contacted the top twelve to gauge their interest in joining the project. Two of them were not able to participate; we sent questionnaires to the remaining ten to help fill in some knowledge gaps. After we received their answers, we re-ranked according to the new data, and we selected the top five for site visits.

Two members of the grant team visited each of the top five sites. Once we were all back from our travels, we reconvened to compare notes. We filled in the partner selection rubric with more details and re-ranked one last time, and this was the order in which we contacted finalists to offer a formal invitation to join the program.

After a rigorous selection process with many great and willing potential partners, we ultimately established partnerships with Boise State University (BSU), the University of Massachusetts Amherst (UMass Amherst), the University of Nevada, Reno (UNR), and the University of North Carolina at Chapel Hill (UNC-Chapel Hill). This book includes contributions from participants at each institution, including librarians, makerspace staff, and faculty.

EXAMPLE COURSES FROM THE MAKER LITERACIES PILOT PROGRAM

By fall 2016 several faculty members from a diverse range of subject disciplines, both on and off the task force, had begun testing the beta competencies as learning outcomes in their courses, with collaboratively developed maker-space assignments custom-designed to foster the desired learning outcomes. Considering that this was the first go at implementing the program and that I was a little rusty, lesson planning was challenging to me. However, I found that participating faculty already had some great ideas, and with the help of the other task force members, we were able to quickly hone in on project prompts for each participating course.

Many of the maker competencies are highly relevant to many undergraduate courses—we designed them to be; but finding the "hook" that also made the FabLab a critical component in achieving those competencies while maintaining a clear disciplinary context was tricky. For example, when a student enrolls in a history class, that individual expects to be learning history. We have to design a project prompt that will not only expose the student to experiential learning in the FabLab but also make sure that the project is relevant to the history course and that the student is learning history. I have to be honest and say that I still find this part difficult. I find that brainstorming with a small group consisting of the instructor and as many program team members as are available and willing to participate leads to the best project prompts because we're all bringing our expertise to the table to problem solve around that issue.

Other major challenges have been measurement of student learning and the lack of available assessment tools to gather the student learning data that we seek. I felt it was of great importance to "design for assessment." This approach incorporates the "backward design" method for curriculum design whereby you figure out what you're going to measure and how you're going to measure it before you even begin to think about the project prompt itself. That way, you design the assignment to "feed" the student learning data you seek into the assessment method or tool. Frankly, things were moving so fast that we just had to have some project prompts ready in time for the semester to begin, and neither the task force nor the participating faculty members could invest the time needed to create great assessment components once the semester began.

By summer 2017, when we conducted our first major assessment of the program, we knew we had a problem. The assessment tools that faculty had been using (if any at all) were not adequately mapped (if at all) to the competencies that we were trying to measure, and we were not able to collect the student learning data we'd hoped for. At this juncture we decided to implement pre– and post–self-assessment surveys for all students enrolled in participating courses (see chapter 5 for more information about this process). We would then have at least one standardized measurement tool for assessing student learning outcomes, independent of the faculty members' assessment tools, that would enable us to compare data across all participating courses. We realized that self-reported student survey data alone wasn't ideal, but it was better than nothing; we also began working more closely with faculty on designing assessment tools and methods that would capture the data desired by the program team. We have mostly used rubrics, but we also try to attend student presentations at which we can directly observe and ask questions related to the competencies. We continue to refine and develop those tools.

In fall 2016 we had three courses ready to give the program a spin. The pilot courses were Dr. Scott Cook's Emerging Technology Studio (Art 4392), Dr. Cedrick May's Afrofuturism course (English 2303), and Dr. Estee Beck's Writing, Rhetoric, and Multimedia Authoring (English 3374). ART 4392 had a mix of upper-level undergraduate students and three graduate students who learned how to use the FabLab's equipment to create an art project (figure 2.1) and then taught others how to use the equipment in an end-of-semester workshop series hosted by the FabLab (see also chapter 5). In ENGL 2303 students contributed to a wiki-based sci-fi universe by creating or embellishing on an existing in-universe character or theme and then creating an object in the FabLab to capture an essential quality of the character or theme. In ENGL 3374 undergraduates conceptualized, designed, and made objects derived from a problem they identified on campus. First, the students wrote about the problems they identified, then they created objects in the FabLab aimed at solving the problems, and, finally, they took professional-quality photographs of their objects.

We continued in spring 2017, adding five new courses to the pilot: Dr. Amanda Alexander's Technology in Art Education (Art 4365), Dr. Christoph Csallner's Object-Oriented Software Engineering (Computer Science and Engineering 3311), Dr. David Sparks's Multiple Teaching Practices in Mathematics and Science (Education 4333), Dr. Estee Beck's Technical Communication (English 3373), and Dr. Bonnie Boardman's Introduction to Industrial Engineering (IE 1205).

Students in ART 4365 used the FabLab's software and hardware resources to complete assignments based on thinking broadly about K–12 classroom problems. Students observed real classroom spaces, formed small groups to address a chosen problem, and worked together to solve the problem using FabLab resources (see also chapter 5).

Students in CSE 3311 undertook a service-learning project by assisting in the development of our in-house FabApp, an open-source suite of software

FIGURE 2.1

A team consisting of Christine Adame (an ART 4392 master's degree student) and several undergraduates focused on learning silk-screen printing using a CNC vinyl cutter in the fall of 2016 and then facilitated an open workshop at UTA Libraries' FabLab. Adame is now an art instructor at UTA and continues to use the FabLab for her own classes.

modules for makerspace resource management. Working in teams, students helped design and implement a ticketing system to log equipment maintenance needs and a system that manages queues of students waiting to use a piece of equipment.

Preservice mathematics and science teachers in EDUC 4333 designed an inquiry-based or project-based learning (PBL) object for use in a mathematics or science classroom. Students conceptualized, designed, and 3D printed their objects in the FabLab. The class culminated with students demonstrating how their objects could be used in an inquiry-based or PBL mathematics curriculum.

Students in ENGL 3373 worked in teams to write case studies of the courses that participated in the fall 2016 Maker Literacies pilot—a meta-assignment for which we encouraged students to seek service learning credit because we planned to use students' case studies to improve the Maker Literacies program. Each case study included the course name and number, a course description, an overview of the maker literacy assignment, and the maker competencies that were selected for assessment.

Students in IE 1205 learned about the design life cycle. Students worked in groups and had a mini-assignment for each stage of the design life cycle that could be completed in the FabLab. Another meta-assignment with potential for service learning credit, the overarching project was to design a training program for new FabLab student assistants, with groups specifically looking at each of the following topics: 3D printer training, laser cutter training, embroidery machine training, motivating new makers to get trained, and identifying trained users.

The preceding summaries are for a handful of the earlier Maker Literacies courses, which I've adapted from our blog. There are more in-depth case studies about these and other courses that have participated in the program throughout this book. We upload all course-related content to the Maker Literacies website and continually add more summaries like these to our blog; I encourage you to visit https://library.uta.edu/makerliteracies/lesson-plans for a full menu of sample curricula that we've developed in the Maker Literacies program.

The program has rapidly continued to grow and evolve, especially thanks to the 2017–2018 IMLS Maker Competencies and the Undergraduate Curriculum planning grant. As of the end of spring 2019, the program had served more than 950 students and thirty-two faculty partners in thirty-eight unique courses, representing thirteen disciplines from five campuses. In fall 2019, at the time of writing this chapter, we added seven new courses to the program along with many repeating courses.

We are presently working through the first phase of our second IMLS grant-funded experience, Maker Immersion: Developing Curriculum Design and Assessment Skills for Academic Makerspace Course Integration (National Leadership Grants for Libraries LG-17-19-0126-19), in which we will identify additional institutional partners and collaboratively develop an immersion program for expanding Maker Literacies even further. By the time this book is published, that grant-funded work will be in full swing with a minimum of twenty new courses added, coming from ten different academic library maker-spaces around the United States, including UTA, many of our existing partners from the first IMLS grant, and the addition of seven new institutional partners.

Members of the initial task force, the subsequent program team, and several of our participating faculty have published and presented at a variety of conferences about the program. Some of these conferences are the International Symposium on Academic Makerspaces, the White House Nation of Makers, the Association of College and Research Libraries, the Texas Library Association, and the American Society for Engineering Management. Further, we have received national recognition for our work by being invited to attend national forums and immersion workshops. Our work has been cited numerous times in the literature, and that number continues to grow. Last, we have been invited to serve on boards, focus groups, and committees based on our experience and expertise in Maker Literacies.

MAKER LITERACIES PROGRAM REQUIREMENTS

What courses currently taught at your university might be a good fit for curricular integration in your academic library makerspace? Are courses already assigning students to use your makerspace? Is there a department or area of study that is underutilizing the makerspace? How might maker technologies be relevant to that discipline? For faculty who wish to include their courses in this program, or to create a program of your own, this section provides an outline of the process.

First, the faculty member, through discussions with makerspace staff and librarians, chooses two or three competencies from our list of maker competencies (see appendix B) to adapt or map as needed to correspond to the instructor's student learning outcomes. Selecting the two or three most applicable competencies is often a challenge. We find that in many cases, faculty members initially identify many more competencies that are relevant to their classes, but through conversation we can help narrow the list to the two or three competencies that will be most relevant, impactful, and measurable for their course.

Second, the faculty member, in partnership with makerspace staff and librarians, creates a new assignment or revises an existing one. Representatives from the Maker Literacies Program Team assist with identifying or creating potential assignments that both fit our program needs and suit the faculty member's own curricular and disciplinary needs and that are realistically accomplishable given the limitations of the specific makerspace, available equipment, and prior knowledge level of students in the class. In this step, we underscore the role of makerspace staff and librarians as partners in the process and not as mere support staff. We not only assist in development of curriculum but also teach software and hardware, provide formative feedback to students in the makerspace, and work side by side with the instructors to assess student work.

Measuring student achievement of these competencies is an important part of this program. The Maker Literacies Program Team has experience with curriculum development, instruction, and assessment of student learning outcomes. We work with faculty to develop a strategy for measuring student learning for their chosen competencies. We are currently creating standardized rubrics that can be applied to each of the competencies. When the rubrics have been tested and finalized, we will require their use in some fashion in all Maker Literacies courses.

Third, the faculty member agrees to select a preferred Creative Commons (CC) license from the Creative Commons website (https://creativecommons. org/choose/). Final versions of curricula will be freely shared on our website with the CC license for redistribution. The faculty member chooses whether to allow adaptations and commercial use of the curriculum, including but not limited to the course name and description, the assignment or project to be completed in the makerspace, the selected maker competencies, the assessment technique used, and the outcomes. This collection will serve as a repository for other institutions that want to build out Maker Literacies programs of their own without having to start from scratch.

Fourth, the faculty member agrees to allow the program team to conduct pre– and post–self-assessment surveys of the students. Individual students may opt out without penalty. Extra credit or participation credit is often awarded for completing the survey (though not for agreeing to participate in the study). The pre-assessment is administered before the students' first visit to the makerspace, and the post-assessment is administered after students have submitted their final projects or other deliverables (performance, oral presentation, etc.). Although some coordination with the instructor is required, the program team administers the surveys with minimal involvement by the instructor.

Fifth, the faculty member and librarian agree to participate in an exhaustive feedback survey or interview after the instructor's first semester in the program. We are serious about constant improvement of the program, and participant feedback is necessary. The participant can choose either the survey or the interview; both include the same questions. This is a one-time obligation; no feedback survey or interview is required after the first semester of participation.

Finally, although planning may take place, we cannot fully implement certain aspects of the program (namely, surveying students) without first gaining institutional review board (IRB) approval. Potential participant institutions should seek this approval early in the process. UTA serves as an IRB of Record for participant institutions, but we have found that about half of our prior and current partners have had to submit requests and be issued their own protocols with their own IRBs, and about half have accepted our IRB as IRB of Record.

I should clarify that these last two points are only mandatory if your institution wants to partner with UTA for data collection and program assessment purposes. Any academic library makerspace can locally create its own version or iteration of a maker literacies program and forgo the feedback survey and IRB approval.

CONCLUSION

In the beginning of this chapter, I talked about my skepticism and doubt about the role of academic libraries in makerspaces and maker literacies. I'll admit, questions and doubts still linger in my mind, though in the four years since we began the program I've found inspiration for my place in all of this, and I'm now an advocate for academic libraries getting involved with makerspaces and maker literacies. Since those early days, and particularly because of the work we were able to complete thanks to the IMLS grant, we have received national recognition for our work. Such recognition demonstrates that others share our desire to implement maker literacies programs in general and specifically in regard to equity, diversity, inclusion, and creation of assessments for measuring the makerspace's impact on student learning.

In hindsight, I now think about my experience leading the effort to build the Maker Literacies program through the same lens that many if not most of our students feel when given an assignment in the makerspace. I had to create something new that I didn't exactly know how to do, and I didn't know what form it would ultimately take. Because of that initial uncertainty I felt very much like an outsider, but through trial and error (and quite a few errors!) and several iterations of improvements over time, with the help of a great team, I was able to persevere.

Transforming from an Ad Hoc Service to an Integrated Curricular Component

Tara Radniecki

The DeLaMare Science and Engineering Library at the University of Nevada, Reno (UNR) has been providing access to makerspace equipment and resources since 2012 with the introduction of the library's first 3D printers and 3D scanners. In the years since, we have expanded our resources to include laser and vinyl cutters, a PCB milling machine, sewing and soldering bars, a variety of hand tools, and more. In addition to providing the equipment, we implemented a unique student-expert staffing model to help users acquire the skills needed to fully utilize the equipment in the space. Each semester two or three student employees, most often studying in the field of engineering, are available at various times throughout the day to assist users in the makerspace. These "Wranglers" conduct one-on-one consultations for 3D modeling, 3D scanning, using the laser cutter, and working with other pieces of equipment in the space. As the resources and support grew in the makerspace, researchers and students started utilizing the space for research and personal projects. Chemists quickly began 3D printing models of molecules they were researching, biomedical graduate students were creating custom tissue baths, and computer science researchers were laser cutting lenses for robots and drones.

Students were also heavily using the space for recreational purposes. The makerspace saw countless personal projects being developed as students created handmade arrow quivers, musical instruments, art of all kinds, and even their own personal 3D printers.

Although there had been a few classes each semester that required use of the makerspace for a particular assignment or extra-credit opportunity, prior to our incorporation of maker competencies the majority of academic work was being done by engineering students who used the space as another workshop to complete their course assignments. Balsa wood bridges (Statics) and foam hovercrafts (Intro to Engineering) are common sights in the space each year. Some art classes have required use of the laser cutter and 3D scanning and printing capabilities, but for the most part, few non-making-focused classes (those outside the engineering and art departments) at the university had created curriculum that required use of the makerspace. And prior to the grant, no courses had worked directly with library makerspace staff to design a lesson plan that would incorporate assessable learning objectives and a rubric into the making-based assignment. Although collaboration had occurred, it was in assignment and project development and makerspace equipment instruction only. Makerspace staff and librarians rarely knew if the outcomes of the assignment were achieved, if instructors were satisfied with the assignment, or if students gained skills that could be transferred elsewhere. Traditionally, the library's makerspace had served the individual ad hoc user.

We had already begun looking for ways to assess the learning that happens in the makerspace and to integrate the makerspace into the university's curricula when UTA approached us about partnering on the Maker Competencies and the Undergraduate Curriculum planning grant from the Institute of Museum and Library Services (IMLS). Although the grant experience was successful for the DeLaMare Library makerspace and participating classes, this chapter will focus on the challenges our space and staff encountered. Originally designed for the ad hoc researcher or student user, the makerspace would need to flex and change in order to accommodate entire classes and to be successful in helping students acquire various learning outcomes through more formal learning experiences. After a brief description of the service model at the time of the grant project, the challenges and action plans to address them will be discussed.

PRIOR SERVICE AND TRAINING MODEL

The makerspace was and remains open during all library hours. During the academic school year, the library is open Sunday through Thursday from 7:30 a.m. until 10 p.m., Friday from 7:30 a.m. until 6 p.m., and Saturday from 11 a.m. until 4 p.m. The makerspace is located on the first floor of the library near a main entrance and comprises approximately 1,600 square feet. This location is amply visible to all users entering the library and has allowed the makerspace to become a staple on the prospective students' tour. Initially, the decision was made to purposely integrate the making technologies and resources into the rest of the library. Instead of being consigned to a closed-off or separated area, the makerspace organically formed around existing library resources including the service desks, traditional paper printers, and twenty-one regular student computer workstations. A 3D printer and laser cutter were tucked into an alcove, another 3D printer lived in the atrium, and the remaining two were near the main service desk. A sewing and soldering bar sat right next to a bank of six computer workstations, and a large format poster printer and flatbed scanner flanked a bank of computers on the other side of the space. For project working surfaces, there were only three six-by-eight-foot tables located in the back of the space near the hand tools and soldering stations. Due to the lack of working area in the actual makerspace, students began working on projects throughout the library wherever there was ample table space. This adaptation was not a problem for two reasons. First, the DeLaMare Library has not been considered a "quiet" library in many years due to a common atrium shared by three of the four floors, resulting in sound traveling easily. Students working on fabrication projects throughout the library can often be loud, but non-making group work is also very common, and noise levels often get louder naturally throughout the day on all floors as more groups come to work together. Library users have not complained about the various types of projects being worked on throughout the building; instead, such activity has become part of the culture of the library. Second, although working on projects outside the makerspace can be messy and potentially damaging to furniture, many of the tables throughout the library were old and already damaged when the makerspace was created. We did not mind students gluing or hammering on tables already in the queue for replacement in the near future.

The DeLaMare Library makerspace began the grant project with an Epilog laser cutter, a Stratasys 3D printer, a LulzBot TAZ 5 3D printer, two Artec 3D scanners, an LPKF PCB milling machine, a large format vinyl cutter, a large format poster printer, a large format paper scanner, and a sewing and soldering bar. A tool cabinet offers a wide variety of hand tools, drills, and some consumables including glue and tape. In addition to these larger pieces of equipment, the makerspace houses a collection of lendable technology available for checkout. This collection contains a wide variety of technologies used in various disciplines supported by the library and is not limited to just those that support fabrication. The collection includes soldering irons, drill bits, Arduino products, Raspberry Pis, virtual reality headsets, Geiger counters, range finders, and more. These items can be checked out by any university student, faculty member, or staff member. Although a very limited number of items are lent strictly for certain classes (e.g., custom circuit kits provided by some engineering courses), the vast majority of items are acquired to support learning, fabrication, innovation, and current research needs in a wide variety of disciplines.

At the time of the grant, the staffing of the makerspace was rather unique in having only two expert student employees (Wranglers) working a combined thirty to forty hours out of the weekly ninety or more hours that the library and makerspace were open. These Wranglers sat at a designated desk near the library's main information desk. They used a dual-screen computer to assist users and helped both walk-in patrons and those who booked an appointment in advance. As the experts in all things makerspace, the Wranglers provided in-depth consultations to anyone wanting to learn about or get assistance with 3D modeling, 3D scanning, using the PCB milling machine, or advanced uses of the vinyl and laser cutters. Wranglers often had a background in engineering and could offer assistance in brainstorming solutions and possibilities for assignment or research project development. They also provided occasional workshops and class instruction when requested and participated in many library outreach activities that involved STEM engagement both on and off campus.

The training for the Wranglers initially mirrored the training given to all library student employees. First, student employees completed basic library training, which included maps, circulation, and other library operations. Next, all library student employees completed basic customer service training. Finally, all students progressed to basic makerspace training, learning how to use the various pieces of equipment first from an online course module and then by going hands-on with the equipment. The hands-on portion was overseen by an existing Wrangler. The training covered basic use of the large format poster printer, the laser cutter, and the vinyl cutter, as well as processing (though not creating) 3D models to be printed.

After that point, new Wranglers would continue their more specialized training. They were asked to use tutorials to learn whatever 3D modeling software we were currently supporting and to begin an informal apprentice relationship with the makerspace manager, learning how to troubleshoot equipment issues as they arose. As the engineering librarian, I discussed the nature of the in-depth consultation with the Wranglers, describing how to conduct a teaching consultation in which the user is empowered to complete the work unattended versus a consultation in which the Wrangler does the work for the user. This training was informal, and no additional reference materials were provided to the Wranglers on the topic. Wranglers were encouraged to draw on their engineering background and work experience and to be creative in assisting patrons to utilize the makerspace and in helping them find solutions to their problems.

During the time of the IMLS grant, the makerspace manager did not oversee any of the student employees and managed only the physical equipment and supplies for the space. Although he spent the majority of his time in the space, he did not provide consultations in 3D modeling, 3D scanning, or other advanced skill sets. The Wranglers instead reported to the library's single student employee supervisor. The student employee supervisor oversaw all aspects of training in both the library and the makerspace with assistance from the makerspace manager when needed for specific makerspace resources.

During all hours that the library was open, a regular library student employee was working in the makerspace area, sitting at the information desk. In addition to providing traditional library services, these student employees provided assistance with processing 3D print jobs, using the laser and vinyl cutters, poster printing, and facilitating the use of various items in the space that require checkout. These students worked in the space even if the makerspace manager or Wranglers were present. As previously mentioned, these students also worked in other areas of the library including circulation and maps. The 3D printers, laser cutter, soldering bar, and hand tools are the most utilized resources in the makerspace. Because all library student employees received basic training on all these resources, they could often meet users' needs without requiring additional assistance from a Wrangler.

IMLS MAKER COMPETENCIES GRANT PROJECT

Before the grant, I had filled a number of roles in the makerspace. Initially, I assisted patrons with using the equipment; created and revamped various logistics tools, including consultation booking and 3D print tracking applications; and contributed to the acquisition of new resources and the maintenance of existing equipment. I also guided the Wranglers on how to give teaching consultations and led many outreach and instructional activities in the space. With the addition of a makerspace manager in mid-2016, my makerspace responsibilities shifted away from equipment maintenance and direct service provision but remained focused on Wrangler consultation scheduling, outreach, and instruction in the space.

During the 2018 spring semester, two classes participated in the IMLS-sponsored grant project and worked with me to incorporate maker competencies into their curriculum. One of the instructors taught a digital art course that had regularly used the makerspace's laser cutter for a course project, and she would be using the same assignment during the grant period. In collaboration with the library, she matched the assignment's learning outcomes to the project's maker competencies and developed additional instruction to address them. This instructor teaches two sections of the course, and approximately thirty students take the course per semester.

The other instructor came from the geology department. Although a heavy user and supporter of the library's more traditional resources and services, she had never assigned coursework that required students to use the makerspace. She chose to incorporate the maker competencies into a 100-level historical geology class. This course maxes out at forty students; however, there are usually about twenty students per semester.

In total, these courses brought approximately fifty students to the makerspace that semester, most of whom had never visited or used the space before. Although the space and service models had served ad hoc users effectively for years, this grant project would be the first real test of assisting entire classes of non-STEM students in navigating the makerspace and achieving measurable learning outcomes.

The art assignment that used the makerspace required only the laser cutter on an introductory level. This limitation meant that all library student employees, Wrangler or otherwise, could assist all students in the course. Individual consultations with a Wrangler were not necessary, and students could work on the makerspace portion of their assignment any time the makerspace was open and the laser cutter was available. Having assisted with this course project for several semesters prior, the library and its employees had become very familiar with the requirements and best practices for successful completion. The project was a lamp cut out of a type of large format card stock on the laser cutter. The basic template to be cut was provided by the instructor, and the students needed to utilize software to create original designs that would be vector cut out of the lamp. The following beta maker competencies (see appendix A) were chosen to be incorporated into the assignment:

- Applies design praxis
- Understands many of the ethical, legal and socioeconomic issues surrounding making

The components of these competencies that were focused on can now be mapped to competencies 3, 6, 7, 8, and 14 in the revised list of maker competencies (see appendix B). The art instructor taught the first competency herself in her class and through the project layout. The assignment guided students through the design process naturally. I am also the Patent and Trademark Resource Center librarian, and I taught a session on intellectual property in the art world and higher education to address some of the legal issues surrounding making. This information was tied to the use of unoriginal designs on students' lamps, how fair use worked in this instance, and how the legal situation regarding intellectual property can change outside the scope of academia.

The historical geology professor created a much more open-ended assignment. Small groups of two to three students each were given a small and incomplete fossil. Some fossils were of animals and others were of plants. Each group was asked to use the makerspace to create a visualization of the fossil (either physical or digital) in order to use it in testing a hypothesis. Such a hypothesis might be that the shape of a coastal fossil's shell diverted water efficiently. The following beta maker competencies (see appendix A) were chosen to integrate into the course:

- Applies design praxis
- Transfers knowledge gained into workforce, community, and real-world situations

These beta competencies can now be mapped to competencies 3, 6, and 12 in the revised list of maker competencies (see appendix B). The assignment required each group of students to meet with a Wrangler to brainstorm what type of visualization of the fossil might be best to test their hypothesis and what piece of equipment in the makerspace it should be created on. All maker competencies were part of the assignment instructions and none was directly taught by the librarian or makerspace staff.

The art instructor was pleased overall with the integration of the maker competencies into her course and discussed how, in general, they helped her think more critically about what she wanted her students to learn and how those outcomes could be acquired. Students were engaged during the intellectual property discussion and were able to make connections to work and examples outside their particular assignment. The chosen maker competencies complemented the existing course's learning outcomes well and aligned naturally with the assignments.

The historical geology instructor invited the library staff to attend the final presentations in which students discussed their projects and the process of using the makerspace. The course was focused more on the students' journey and learning during the process and less on the final physical project outcome. Some students expressed that although initially the project and the makerspace seemed daunting, in the end they wished they had been exposed to the makerspace earlier in their academic careers. They expressed gratitude for being exposed to such technologies and for the high level of assistance provided by the Wranglers. The following semester, one of the students came back to share her work with the students about to begin their assignments and offered words of encouragement and excitement.

CHALLENGES FOR THE MAKERSPACE

Although both courses had successful experiences with the grant project, our makerspace and staff did face some challenges.

Staffing

As the coordinator of the grant project at UNR, I was involved in the grant writing process and was very familiar with the grant's goals and the maker competencies to be implemented and, as a liaison librarian, was experienced in collaborating with faculty to create educational materials such as learning outcomes and assignments. At this point in time, the makerspace manager played no role in and had no experience with creating formal and assessable educational opportunities within the makerspace. He instead was asked to focus on equipment maintenance, assisting with walk-in users of the space, and providing as-needed training and guidance to Wranglers and other library student employees working in the space.

The two Wranglers working for the library at that time focused on walk-in users and individuals who prebooked consultations to learn how to 3D model, 3D scan, and use other, more complex maker resources. Although all staff involved were eager to assist in the project, we felt that by not giving the makerspace manager and Wranglers more training in what the grant was hoping to accomplish, opportunities to help students acquire more mastery of certain maker competencies were missed.

All geology students were required to meet with a Wrangler. I told the Wranglers ahead of time what the assignment was and the basic idea behind the grant's goals but gave them few details about the specific competencies we were hoping the students would acquire and how the Wranglers could help the students acquire those competencies. The Wranglers were to brainstorm ideas with the students about how they could utilize the maker equipment and services in order to create a visualization and assist the students in learning something new about their fossil. Initially, the participating faculty and I believed that designing the assignment to incorporate the maker competencies, either through specific assignment instructions such as "analyze a problem and develop possible solutions" or through additional direct instruction by the professor addressing particular maker competencies, would be adequate in helping students acquire those competencies. However, conversations with the Wranglers and some participating students revealed some difficulty in brainstorming potential solutions for the geology course, thus hampering students' movement through the process required to attain the competencies. Although struggling is often part of the learning and design processes, I felt that had the Wranglers had a firmer grasp of the desired maker competencies themselves, they could have become co-instructors and acted as another point of support for the students, helping them work through the design and prototyping processes with more confidence. Although the Wranglers are natural problem solvers and work with users from a wide variety of backgrounds, it seems a lack of formal training in both the maker competencies and pedagogical practices may have hindered them from playing a larger role in the students' overall class success. We cannot, of course, provide Wranglers with in-depth, subject-specific knowledge for every discipline on campus, but we can teach them the maker competencies and particular pedagogical skills and practices that will allow them to help teach those competencies to others.

Our limited number of Wranglers also proved to be a challenge during the grant. Having only two Wranglers who worked thirty to forty hours combined a week and served an existing large user population beyond the participating courses made it difficult for all students to meet with them to brainstorm ideas and meet course deadlines. Depending on the class schedules and preferences of the Wranglers, we may only offer their services during daytime hours during the week and limited times on the weekend. Often the Wranglers can be prebooked for their entire shift, making them unavailable for walk-ins. Their popularity among community members, students, and researchers nearly caps out their existing staffing model, making direct curriculum involvement challenging.

Space Concerns

During the time of the grant, the makerspace occupied approximately 1,600 square feet of the first floor of the library. The center housed a regular library information desk and the Wrangler consultation desk. Makerspace equipment radiated from that point around the room. There were also nineteen computers occupying the same space. As previously mentioned, initially, library leaders wanted to integrate the makerspace as much as possible into the rest of the library to prevent a separate entity from being formed. This was an effective way to send the message that the whole library is a place for making. Although this arrangement helped develop the collaborative, inventive, and casual atmosphere the library now has, the lack of a larger open floor plan within the makerspace itself prevents any single class larger than approximately ten students from using the space at the same time. For the grant-related courses, as well as any other courses on campus with makerspace-based assignments, an initial tour of the makerspace is given by one of our librarians, and the real work is done by the students outside traditional class time. Ideally, a hands-on instruction session could happen within the makerspace where there is opportunity for learning with and from makerspace staff, the course instructor, and peers.

IMPLEMENTING A NEW SERVICE MODEL

In light of the difficulties just described, we have begun to explore different service models to better meet the needs of classes and our ad hoc users. A makerspace director position was created to oversee the makerspace manager and help guide the assessment and revision of current service models and resources. My familiarity with the grant and makerspace pedagogy allowed me to move into this position (while retaining engineering liaison responsibilities) and help guide the future direction of the space to better serve all users, especially those courses wishing to integrate the space into their curriculum. This position also provides support to the makerspace manager in order to allow him to flex his time to further develop the employee training process, realign the physical space to meet user needs, and begin to work directly with teaching faculty.

Student Staffing

Beginning in the summer of 2019, all students who work in the makerspace will be classified and trained as Wranglers. This model will ensure that every person working in the makerspace area is trained to provide the highest quality and most knowledgeable assistance. Instead of having only two Wranglers working limited hours throughout the week, the makerspace will increase the total number of student employees to nine. One Wrangler will work during the hours the makerspace manager is in the space, and two Wranglers will work during all other times the library is open and the makerspace manager is not present. During these times, one Wrangler will be available for prebooked consultations while the other will provide assistance for walk-in users. The additional staffing and strategic availability of prebooked consultations will increase the availability of Wranglers greatly, making it easier for both ad hoc makerspace users and those in classes that require meeting with a Wrangler as part of an assignment. All Wranglers will now report to our makerspace manager because they will no longer have any responsibilities for services in the larger library. This direct reporting line will allow Wranglers to communicate more effectively and quickly in addressing issues as they arise instead of waiting until the next Wrangler comes onto a shift later in the day or the next day.

Training for the Wranglers will also be substantially revised. Previous training efforts for all student employees, both library and Wrangler, was thorough in regard to equipment and how to use it for various basic projects. The training lessons were delivered online initially through a Canvas module. Unfortunately, these modules tended to get lengthy because of all the information necessary for safe and effective use of various pieces of equipment. After completing the modules, new student employees were asked to make consultation appointments with existing Wranglers to learn more about the equipment, tips and tricks, and common problems and to go hands-on to make something. This system worked well for several reasons. Students could schedule appointments when it was most convenient for them, they learned from their peers, and they created strong work relationships with the Wranglers and each other through a common experience. However, the system was quite informal and didn't guarantee that all new student employees would receive exactly the same information, depending on which Wrangler they worked with and what happened to be going on in the makerspace that day, which would often influence what the Wrangler taught. The online modules ensured that all student employees achieved the same basic understanding, but the modules could not capture the tips and tricks and advanced methods that Wranglers were sharing during follow-up consultations. When expanding from two to potentially nine Wranglers, we knew we would need to capture more of that vital information being exchanged during peer consultations and change the format of training in order to effectively teach a larger number of new student employees.

Moving forward, the training will still utilize existing online modules and will expand them to include the more advanced skills and knowledge required for Wrangler work. However, follow-up training will involve entire cohorts of new employees learning from the makerspace manager and existing

Wranglers in a group setting, following predesigned lesson plans. These lesson plans will be created with input from existing Wranglers in order for incoming student employees to learn the same information regardless of who teaches the session or what is going on in the makerspace that day. The modules will be revamped to include information literacy skills when applicable. Maker competencies will also be taught in a stand-alone lesson to help the Wranglers understand the larger mission and goals of the makerspace: to help students learn skills transferable beyond the project they are building at any given point in time. With this knowledge, the Wranglers can play a larger role when classes are mapped to maker competencies and can help guide students as they achieve the desired learning outcomes.

Additional training will also be developed to prepare Wranglers to give teaching consultations. In the makerspace, consultations are advertised as teaching and co-working sessions in which users can learn various skills from a Wrangler, including 3D modeling, 3D scanning, laser cutting, and more depending on their needs. In the past, our Wranglers were simply encouraged to teach users what the Wranglers thought those users needed to know. However, these consultations and the determination of the users' needs mirror the traditional reference interview. Existing training for peer research consultants (working elsewhere in the library) will be used as a guide to flesh out a more comprehensive consultation training program that will empower Wranglers with the skills they need to determine what a user really needs and how Wranglers can help teach those skills most effectively.

User Training

Training for new users of the space will also be implemented in the coming year. Currently, users new to the makerspace are given a brief and informal introduction to each piece of equipment they would like to use. For example, a student wanting to use the laser cutter for the first time would ask an employee for assistance. That employee would ask what the user would like to make and then show the individual how to do so. Although this approach has worked well for several years and creates no barrier to use, as the number of users increases, it will become a burden to constantly be training users in small aspects of all the equipment instead of teaching them more in a single session. The one-on-one method also does not guarantee that new users are learning the same thing from each employee, including vital safety information, because what they are being taught is very project-specific. And finally, incoming new users are not necessarily learning all the interesting ways each piece of equipment can be utilized if they are just being taught how to complete a specific project. If they have a deeper understanding of how each machine works, they can potentially move beyond introductory-level projects, like engraving a water bottle, to more advanced making, like developing creative solutions to research problems.

At the time of this writing we have not finalized how this new user training program will be implemented. We anticipate that in-person training sessions for each major piece of equipment in the space will be offered several times a week, taught by either the makerspace manager or a Wrangler. Those with access to the university's learning management system will get access to an online module for reference after the training, and those without access will receive a physical reference booklet. Once the training has been completed, a note will be placed on the user's library account stating that the person has been trained and is welcome to reserve and use the equipment.

Physical Space

The physical footprint of the makerspace was recently increased from roughly 1,600 to 2,030 square feet to beta test a larger working area for the fall 2019 semester, allowing us to accommodate larger classes in the space. Working with the library's building operations supervisor, we temporarily moved thirteen computers out of the makerspace area to other locations in the library in order to provide more space for worktables and to allow for rearranging of the equipment. A dedicated space for each equipment type was established to provide for better traffic flow. Previously, soldering, sewing, and heat pressing all shared a single space, and other large items, like the 3D printers and laser cutter, were simply placed where dedicated circuits were available. Because space is always at a premium in libraries, this expansion was only made possible by reimaging and rearranging several other areas in the library to be more efficient with their use of space in order for the library to not lose computing resources. The additional square footage will provide more room to hold at least small formal classes. In order to have more classes implement maker competencies, it will be important to provide enough room in the makerspace for entire classes to work and learn together instead of having students come separately on their own time outside class.

The layout of the service points was also evaluated. During the time of the grant, a service desk sat in the front center of the space, flanked by another desk serving as the consultation desk for Wranglers. Although this arrangement provided a central and visible point of service, it took up a large area and created a bottleneck to get to the majority of the makerspace, which sat behind the desks. When users walked into the space, they had difficulty seeing what resources were available and may have been unsure about whether they were welcome to walk behind the desks and use all the resources.

The service desks also served as anchors, keeping our Wranglers inadvertently tethered to them. Although this concept is not inherently bad, we wanted to create a space in which our Wranglers felt encouraged to walk around and engage with users instead of sitting and waiting to be asked a question. We wanted to provide a more organic and less formal atmosphere of co-working and co-making. Getting the Wranglers more engaged physically would also give them a better sense of what is happening in the space, which would allow them to give assistance faster and become aware of safety issues more quickly.

To address these various issues, the Wrangler service desk was removed completely. Instead, two workstations sitting side by side on a table now serve as the consultation area. The side-by-side setup makes it easier to teach new users how to utilize maker software by allowing the Wrangler to demonstrate on one computer and then have the user engage in active learning by completing the steps on the other computer. The consultation area is located in a corner of the space where it was not appropriate to place other equipment. The consultation area no longer blocks pathways in the makerspace and is no longer an anchor point for employees. The service desk was pulled to the side of the room, opening up the middle of the floor for worktables and natural walkways throughout the makerspace. The service desk remains highly visible but is no longer a barrier to access to the makerspace.

Equipment Acquisition

Having formal course assignments in the makerspace that needed to be completed by up to forty students also showed the limitations caused by having only one of a particular piece of equipment. The art students needed to use the laser cutter for their project. Although the geology students were given the option to use any piece of equipment in the makerspace, several groups chose the laser cutter for various reasons, including that it is beginner-friendly and can be used flexibly with a variety of materials. This heavy use on top of our normal laser cutter traffic meant the machine was fully booked for days at a time. Walk-ins were unable to use the machine, and the limited number of bookings available meant that some students were scrambling to get their project done by the deadline.

A second, less powerful laser cutter has been purchased that will still meet the needs of a majority of users and help the makerspace increase, and potentially double, the number of users. As course use continues to expand, the makerspace will need to identify other pieces of equipment that should be duplicated in order to facilitate more concurrent use. Beginning in fall 2019, the makerspace began collecting usage statistics on a wider variety of resources, including nonreservable items like hand tools and soldering stations, to help make these acquisition decisions.

Courses that use the makerspace for assignments, like those participating in the grant, also inform the acquisition decisions of the space. Knowing that courses will use certain pieces of equipment to achieve learning outcomes makes the acquisition decision, and the financial ask to administration, much easier. Also, as more course and project syllabi are freely shared through the grant's web page, staff can make informed decisions about which types of equipment used elsewhere might best facilitate both making in general and the acquisition of maker competencies at UNR.

CONCLUSION

Participating in the grant allowed our makerspace to critically examine its role in student achievement and the acquisition of transferable maker competencies. In wanting to take the next step in our evolution and support formal curriculum, we became aware of several opportunities for growth and change that will allow the makerspace to support large populations of users in assessable ways.

Those of us who work in makerspaces know that learning happens in them every single day. But the tricky part is assessing that learning and determining how it is impacting the student's overall success. For the DeLaMare Library's makerspace, the next step before we can begin formally assessing is to create a space that facilitates larger group work and contributes in meaningful ways to the actual course design and instruction. Achieving these goals not only will involve physical space changes and student staffing adjustments, but the full-time staff will also have to shift their roles in order to become true collaborators to those faculty wishing to utilize the makerspace as a learning lab for their courses.

Inclusion by Design

Amy Vecchione

aker competencies are critical for courses in every discipline. Within the scope of higher education, many individuals have the perspective that makerspaces involve all STEM disciplines, yet making is a crucial aspect of work in the humanities, the arts, education, and the social sciences. Developing an inclusive practice to attract and retain faculty and students from all areas is critical to the success of a makerspace. When we set out to create the MakerLab at Boise State University, we designed the space with inclusion and equity in mind. Through our process of working with history and philosophy faculty through the Maker Literacies grant from the Institute of Museum and Library Services (IMLS), we were also able to help create a new competency incorporating the concepts of diversity, equity, and inclusion so that these principles could be more broadly acknowledged and adopted by other makers.

When designing any space, one must consider the audience. A well-designed makerspace attracts people from diverse backgrounds, disciplines, and identities; when these teams work together, they produce better results. An early question for the MakerLab at Boise State University was "How can we design a space to allow individuals from every major to come together and solve problems?" This competency is necessary and should be considered in the design of the space and in the instructional techniques that are used so that diverse makerspace teams can focus on collaboration, teamwork, and problem solving. This process allows transdisciplinary teams to achieve some incredible projects and ideas. This practice of developing an inclusive makerspace is precisely what will connect the humanities, arts, and social sciences into the makerspace. Students from all disciplines can then, in turn, better acquire aptitudes related to equity and inclusion when working in such intentionally designed spaces.

Making should include aspects of certain values to add meaning to the work being accomplished. As mentioned in chapter 2, two of the primary goals of the IMLS planning grant were to test and assess the list of beta maker competencies in a variety of library makerspace settings and to ultimately revise the list of competencies to enable its broad applicability for all library makerspaces interested in integrating curricular development, despite potentially varied sizes, staffing models, equipment selections, geographic locations, and user bases. When we began working with this list of maker competencies, we connected with two faculty members who led assignments in history and philosophy courses. Through the process of developing maker curriculum and comparing the students' learning goals to the competencies list, this grant collaboration at Boise State University led to the development of competency 13: "Be mindful of the spectrum of cultural, economic, environmental, and social issues surrounding making." As discussed in the following text, makers should often consider sustainability, equity of access, and ethics when creating something new, and through the incorporation of this new competency, faculty and librarians are now more cognizant of teaching and emphasizing these important issues.

ABOUT BOISE STATE UNIVERSITY

Boise State University is a doctoral-granting research university in the northwest. Located in Boise, Idaho, the university is situated in an isolated region of southwest Idaho. Boise is unique in Idaho for being a hub of entrepreneurial creativity and recreational diversity.

ORIGINS OF THE MAKERLAB

Albertsons Library's MakerLab aims to be a radically inclusive space on Boise State's campus with the full spirit of the core values of the American Library Association (ALA) in mind. We aim to support student success by providing access and ensuring equal accessibility to resources for all library users.[1] The library also strives to provide all the resources needed by the community we serve, especially in light of equity, diversity, and inclusion. We hold consultations with our users about creating new information that benefits the public good, while also offering services that aim to do the same. As a result, we try to solve problems within the communities we serve, as ALA's social responsibilities core value states:

> The broad social responsibilities of the American Library Association are defined in terms of the contribution that librarianship can make in ameliorating or solving the critical problems of society; [and in] support for efforts to help inform and educate the people of the United States on these problems and to encourage them to examine the many views on and the facts regarding each problem.[2]

The Albertsons Library MakerLab was established in 2015 with support from the Albertsons Library administration, faculty, staff, and students. The purpose of the MakerLab was to provide access to emerging technologies to all students, staff, and faculty at the university, a facility "open to anyone regardless of their discipline."[3] The intent was to create not only a space for tools but also a place for students to connect and have conversations that lead to the creation of new information—a place "where students can apply things they've learned in the classroom or found through research, experiment and experience failure in an informal setting."[4]

The MakerLab currently provides three primary services: access to a variety of selected technologies, coaching and safety training to use these technologies, and instruction for courses with regard to the makerspace. The instruction program became more robust by working with the Maker Literacies grant team to help establish a formal process of creating instruction plans in different disciplines. Although we had been creating instruction tailored to each instructor's request, the process of using the maker competencies helped us better target and understand some of the goals and outcomes to develop in designing the instruction so that we were actively teaching in a transformational style and not solely focusing on the technical aspects of a piece of equipment. Library faculty at Albertsons Library have provided instruction since the inception of the makerspace, marking four years of increasing demands on maker-related instruction; this history of curricular involvement in our space was one of the primary reasons we were selected as grant partners and provided us with a baseline against which to more substantively assess the incorporation of the competencies. Since 2015 the maker instruction program has grown from between three and five instruction sessions to approximately twenty maker instruction sessions per semester. In addition, even more classes use the makerspace to complete their work, though not all request a formal instruction session to complete their assignments.

We worked early on to develop our own homegrown instruction with the collaborations from the other universities in the Make School initiative. Learning from others across the country about how they design instruction was helpful and enabled us to get started. Working with the team at the University of Texas at Arlington (UTA), we were able to further develop our instruction program. Finally, we worked with Stephanie Milne Lane, a graduate student at the University of Washington, to completely revise our instruction program, which is now formalized. We host lesson plans on our website and use the ACRL *Framework for Information Literacy for Higher Education* to design the best possible lesson plans with our faculty. We work with more than thirty faculty members across campus each semester and incorporate new practices and pedagogies as we continually seek to improve our work. This improvement includes growing the number of users, courses, and activities in our MakerLab. The nature of the inclusion by design practice has led to this growth.

MAKER-RELATED PEDAGOGY

The MakerLab has a high degree of faculty involvement, and developing our instructional pedagogy has been essential to developing our maker instruction program. We relied heavily on the book *Meaningful Making* to generate ideas for curricula we can use in any discipline.[5] Ultimately, we found several concepts and ideas that helped guide us: maker assignments are a natural fit with authentic assessment via maker portfolios; experiential learning can honor all users' prior learning; tinkering can lead to innovation; and maker conversations facilitate the creation of new information in our communities.

By leveraging existing faculty relationships and by being inclusive and talking about making from an ethical perspective, we were able to connect the makerspace to the social sciences, arts, and the humanities very early on. Working with Dr. Leslie Madsen in the Department of History, we printed a life mask of Abraham Lincoln digitized from the Smithsonian. As our 3D printing capabilities increased, we printed additional life masks. As a result, Dr. Madsen now has a series of these 3D prints in her office, attesting to how much the 3D printing process and our knowledge about it have improved over time. This project led to many positive correlations.

History department faculty felt more empowered to get involved with makerspaces and making in their curriculum. We worked with several other faculty in this department to design assignments with their classes. These experiences led to many encounters with yet more history faculty members, three of whom took part in a faculty learning community we offered on making and makerspaces. They continue to use these skills, competencies, and resources in their courses. As a result, we have been able to reach a broader group of individuals. This extension of service boosts the makerspace community's ability to talk about the historical making experience, especially within the context of a population's creation and use of objects.

Connecting with Dr. Stephen Crowley in the Philosophy Department to model the creation of new information led ultimately to helping him develop a maker assignment on the philosophy of science. The students enrolled in this course worked to re-create experiments performed by scientists. In this process, the students created new information.

In the two pilot courses for the IMLS grant, faculty librarians partnered once more with Dr. Madsen and Dr. Crowley to help facilitate successful maker course assignments. As a result of these professors' careful and thoughtful feedback, we were able to fully develop the competency outlined here:

Be mindful of the spectrum of cultural, economic, environmental, and
    social issues surrounding making
    a. express awareness of diversity and inclusion when identifying
       unmet needs
    b. consider sustainability when making, including upcycling and
       recycling materials

c. scrutinize the ethical implications of making

Through the process of reflection, students who engaged in Dr. Madsen's history course (Women in America: The Western Experience) were able to better articulate some of the more nuanced aspects of historical concepts. The students were tasked with studying a pair of shoes from the Idaho State Historical Society's collections; using the information from their investigations, they then created an object that would reveal the history of women in Idaho. This task led them to understand more deeply some design choices. For example, why were certain shoes made with different types of materials at different times? This question helped lead processes of inquiry in the makerspace. By engaging with the space, which had been designed to best serve these students, and by working with the competencies directly, the students had a transformative experience of learning.

Professor Madsen's assignment, entitled "In Her Shoes," required students to develop new and contextualized information regarding the cultural and historical significance of shoes that women wore in different time periods. Students scanned, analyzed, made digital models, and created multimedia projects about their assigned pair of shoes from the historical society's collection. Through the process of working with digital and historical objects, the students created new information, new interpretations, and new understandings about this content. The students made websites, videos, and interactive modules that helped other individuals learn about selected topics. As the students scanned shoes and evaluated and created these multimedia examples through the frame of maker competencies, their understanding increased. The lens of creation is different from that of a traditional paper writing assignment, and, as a result, the learning must be authentic in a different way.

Within this course assignment, students were confronted with issues of context and labels in historical research. What does gender mean in the context of shoes? How were shoes created? Students had to confront a diverse range of opinions and consider the needs of many to understand the greater context. This assignment also led students on a journey of considering the materials that were used in the construction of the shoes, prompting discussions about sustainability and the ethical implications within this context. Some shoes required more expensive and environmentally unsound practices to create, while others used more sustainable practices. Who wore which, and why? What were the purposes of these shoes? At the time of the grant pilot, no maker competency comprehensively covered the ethical inquiry that these history students were engaging in—a skill that is certainly transferable beyond the scope of this project; perceiving this omission led us to fill that gap through the creation of competency 13.

Dr. Crowley led his Philosophy of Science students, who came from a variety of backgrounds, on a journey to explore Galileo's inclined plane. Galileo used this item to establish the theory of gravity. Students used their prior learning along with social, environmental, and historical contexts to obtain new information. Because no one knows how Galileo calculated the passing of time in this context, the students had to discuss this mystery among themselves and conduct research, in the process creating their own new versions of this work. In this course, students considered many alternate theories regarding gravity. In the makerspace, they purchased items that would have been available in Galileo's time and built items that they thought would help Galileo understand the theories he wrote about and espoused. The class built a giant ramp and a variety of counting mechanisms to try to measure the speed with which an object went down the ramp. They had to trust one another and honor each other's diverse perspectives within the context of making in order to form a full opinion on this topic. Together, using unique perspectives, they were able to solve the problem for themselves.

In both of these contexts, the students worked together from a variety of backgrounds to use both their experiential knowledge and the content from the course to create new information. Each student considered the ethical issues surrounding science and making and needed to be aware of the perspectives of others throughout the process of creating course deliverables.

In addition, by creating a makerspace that serves everyone, our employee team was able to better serve these students because we were prepared for their nuanced questions. Some traditional makerspaces may cater to groups that are already familiar with making and emerging technology lingo and vernacular; our makerspace, however, has worked with a lot of individuals who are not familiar with emerging technologies at all. In fact, some are slightly resistant to having to learn these new skills and don't understand the applicability or relevance of the makerspace to their course. By working with a range of students, from those who have no familiarity with maker tools to those who visit repeatedly, we grow more nimble and are better able to serve all students. It is especially poignant when our staff can help connect student learning in the makerspace to students' previous experiences, as was the case with these two courses.

Just as important, this awareness and valuing of prior knowledge mean it is easier for us to work with individual faculty in departments from all across the campus, not just from STEM-related fields. Ultimately, every discipline creates new information in different ways. Some of our more significant collaborations, outside philosophy and history, have involved education, psychology, and art faculty and students. By being open, creative, and collaborative with the faculty, and by being inclusive of all disciplines, we can set the stage for greater makerspace participation. Partnering with these faculty led to thoughtful discussion regarding maker competencies.

HONORING PRIOR LEARNING

As evidenced by the history and philosophy coursework just described, the MakerLab strives to honor the prior experience of the makers and users of the space, demystifying making and creating a space for failure. As unique spaces, makerspaces have the capacity to lower the barrier for access into STEM and innovation and design principles. When we honor prior learning, we allow a greater number of individuals to access the space.

Individuals often come into the makerspace with course projects or passion projects in mind. They arrive with all their own experiences and knowledge, from times when they have repaired or fixed something and from their expertise in their discipline—the content they acquire in their courses. By honoring their prior learning, the space can become more inclusive, and we can demonstrate that the creators can also embrace this competency in their own work.

There are many ways to foster the concept of prior learning in the makerspace both within traditional instruction methods and informally when teaching. The most important aspect to keep in mind is that folks may already be familiar with the topic you are approaching. It's critical when engaging with learners to ask them what they already know about a topic. It is possible that they have already learned project management or acquired a specific maker skill by working with the same technology, background that can be straightforward. But what about transference? That can be trickier to identify.

In making, a variety of skills can transfer from other areas. When describing concepts and skills to students, be sure to include other areas of life in which they might have previously encountered a similar concept. These areas can include, but would not be limited to, cooking and baking, working on cars, dealing with health care issues, or any situation that required problem solving. Sharing anecdotal stories regarding the maker competencies allows students to consider their own stories and realize how to apply their past experiences to a newer, possibly unfamiliar technology or creative process.

CULTURALLY RESPONSIVE AND INCLUSIVE PRACTICES

As stated earlier, the foundations of the maker competency to consider the "spectrum of cultural, economic, environmental, and social issues surrounding making" ought to be included in the design and practices of a makerspace itself, not just thought of as a learning outcome for the courses run within the space. With this integration in mind, leaders of makerspaces can consider adopting certain culturally responsive and inclusive practices while teaching others how to do the same.

Biases, stereotype threats, and generalizations are important first factors to consider. How are individuals within a makerspace engaging in professional communication? Are some individuals being referred to by name or by some other quality? How are we talking to individuals? Professionalizing the makerspace by encouraging employees to consider their own biases and then challenging them through training programs is essential to helping students learn to do the same. At Boise State University, we ask each employee to take the seven-day Bias Cleanse focusing on racial, gender, and anti-LGBTQIA+ biases offered by the Kirwan Institute for the Study of Race and Ethnicity at The Ohio State University and to participate in trainings offered by the Gender Equity Center on campus. Customer service should be broadly understood as dealing with others using the "platinum rule": treating others as they want to be treated while adhering to the safety policies of the makerspace.

A primary goal of librarians in higher education makerspaces should be to connect with faculty in all disciplines, whether or not those disciplines or faculty members consider "making" an essential activity. Each major and discipline works to create new information; therefore, many assignments rely on the use of maker competencies and maker-type emerging technologies to discover new information. Librarians can help bridge that gap in understanding.

Who is actually using your makerspace? Makerspace employees are responsible for evaluating who is using your space and for reaching out to those individuals who are not represented in the space. In higher education, it is possible to obtain data showing who is using equipment and to request de-identified data to evaluate this information.

Honoring experiential learning is key to showing individuals that they are already makers. Our makerspace hosts many conversations about who a maker is (all humans are makers) and what "making" is. These conversations take place both formally and informally. Individuals who walk into the space with their projects naturally discuss making as well as their projects. Most projects are inspired by personal interests and passions, which tend to be tied to individual identities and experiences. Because of the nature of this kind of making, the conversations about who can sew (anyone) and who can code (anyone) happen regularly. In addition, we lead these conversations in instruction sessions to meet an instructor's objective to demystify making or to help learners see themselves as people who tinker or make.

Every instruction session requires that we ask students to define a makerspace as a group. We then ask the group to define *making*. One key anchor activity involves discussing the most recent thing students made. Some learners made coffee or a sandwich, whereas others worked on a project for their house or their car. Individuals who work full time often have an example of something they made in their working environment, such as a nurse who improvised a splint to improve the pain level of a patient. By exploring and broadening the definition of *making*, individuals unfamiliar with the makerspace will begin to see themselves on a greater trajectory of making. They can see that with each thing they made, they followed steps, failed, and learned something new. They can describe how they consulted with others—coworkers, family members, and friends—to garner new information about the solution they are implementing. If a person can make a new cookie recipe, that person can 3D print. It's all about following a series of steps, gaining comfort with ambiguity, and trusting the community of learners in the makerspace.

When trying to find something to 3D print, some users might discover that their culture is not represented on the website Thingiverse or other, similar open-source repositories. A critical practice is to teach maker employees how to facilitate the creation of new items that can be 3D printed or created out of vinyl or cut with a CNC and then shared through these repositories. Our student employees do this all the time—and teach others how to do so. As we teach our employees how to design, they then teach all the users how to do so. Individuals who are designing to meet their needs represent the best-case scenario for making in higher education contexts.

CONCLUSION

At the root of this work, practices must match the method of delivery and content. If we are going to teach undergraduates how to design ethically, we must also design ethically. When we do so, we are able to transform the kinds of learning that can take place within a library makerspace. In addition, through the processes of designing this instruction and designing the makerspace, we can create an inclusive environment in which individuals from all backgrounds, majors, and disciplines can work together. In diversity of thought we can find promising work to transform our theories and find solutions to common problems.

NOTES

1. "Access to Library Resources and Services," American Library Association, http://www.ala.org/advocacy/intfreedom/access.
2. "Core Values of Librarianship," American Library Association, http://www.ala.org/advocacy/intfreedom/corevalues.
3. Tracy Bicknell-Holmes, "Why a MakerLab in a Library?," Boise State University, https://library.boisestate.edu/wp-content/uploads/2017/06/Why-a-MakerLab-in-a-Library.pdf.
4. Bicknell-Holmes, "Why a MakerLab in a Library?"
5. Paulo Bliksein, Sylvia Libow Martinez, and Heather Allen Pang, *Meaningful Making: Projects and Inspirations for Fab Labs and Makerspaces* (Torrance, CA: Constructing Modern Knowledge Press, 2016).

Collaborative Curriculum Codevelopment for Studio-Based Learning

Morgan Chivers

n a previous iteration of myself, I was an adjunct faculty member teaching sculpture and design courses to undergraduate art majors. Throughout those formative experiences in the studio-based classroom, I was concerned less with the actual projects students were making than with their learning of new skills, both technical and cerebral. A student's portent for future successes—whether as a professional artist or as an adult human enabled with critical thinking and refined seeing skills working in any other field—is not determined by the merits of any individual work of art; my primary goal as an educator has always been the opening of minds to become legitimately inquisitive about the motivations, materials, and methods we bring to the creative act.

As anyone who has spent time teaching is well aware, there is a persistent "discrepancy" between an instructor's perception of a student's growth and the measurable results shown through tests and assessment strategies.[1] Some students understand how to succeed in the system of our modern educational bureaucracy more than they comprehend the actual significance of the content supposedly imparted; other students do not trust themselves or the assessment scenario sufficiently to provide an accurate record of their knowledge as it exists in the context of their actual life, beyond the anxious moment of the test.

This is true within virtually any class, studying any subject.

Educators who have experience leading advanced courses with open-ended, student-determined projects will also know the frustration and disappointment that come with witnessing students alter promising ideas when they realize it would require them to expend an intimidating amount of time and effort to learn a new technique. After a few semesters of struggling against this tendency, I started reorienting my syllabi to explicitly encourage risk-taking and demonstrable experimentation over the portfolio-readiness of completed projects and restructuring my assignments to require that every student learn to use every major tool we had available to us in that course's lab space. I paired this new approach with a mental framing device that I wish had been shared with me in many of my undergraduate art courses: think of the first assignment or two as technical exercises and save the art for the final project.

Awash in the post-modernist embrace of de-skilled art aesthetics, far too many students sell themselves short with half-hearted attempts to explain away the obvious signs of being unfamiliar with a material or process as though their lack of developed craftsmanship was a conceptual choice. This is not a criticism of de-skilled art itself; my issue is with the disingenuous use of the aesthetics of certain forms of outsider art (while within a university art department) as a screen to distract from unpracticed skills (especially within an academic program explicitly intended to impart practiced skills). I believe we too often set students up for this kind of posturing by expecting meaningful work from immature art students on a specific schedule, rather than encouraging them to embrace the educated ethos of making earnest experiments not intended to be defended as art. The point here is that attempting both simultaneously runs the risk of accomplishing neither efficiently. Creating space for exploration frees the student to flex her capabilities with various workflows, be honest about her successes and failures during conversation and critique, and find affinities for materials and tools she would have likely shied away from if left to her own predilections or concerns about ensuring project success as a path to good grades. Full disclosure: my own artistic practice is predominantly conceptual; the intellectual work of conceptual rigor requires mentoring and practice at least as much as technical proficiencies.

STUDIO ARTS SKILL-BUILDING AND ASSESSMENT

It was with this mindset that I led my intermediate sculpture class through the first third of a semester with detailed, hands-on instruction for the safe and proper use of each equipment technology in the wood and metals shops; I supplied all the requisite materials and assigned a defined object that would necessitate the competent use of almost every piece of equipment. Purely for my own awareness of the experience level the incoming students were bringing with them, I asked them to spend some time during the first day of class filling out an informal paper survey on their familiarity with the equipment and processes we would be using. This information helped me understand how foundational to get with each training session. At the end of the semester, almost on a lark, I asked them to fill out the same survey again, without showing them their responses from sixteen weeks prior.

When I compared learners' end-of-semester surveys with their beginning-of-semester surveys, I was more than a bit surprised to see that aforementioned discrepancy in perceptions of student growth staring back at me: if the results of the surveys were to be believed, several students who had done quite well in the course had claimed rather low levels of proficiency compared with their classmates who had not demonstrated as much skill, while many students had evidently lost quite a bit of knowledge about the tools and techniques they seemed to be using successfully!

I thought about this paradox for a while and wondered if it might have something to do with the Dunning-Kruger effect, whereby those with rudimentary knowledge of a topic assume they are more knowledgeable than they actually are due to their ignorance about the profundity of information and nuance in which experts on that topic are well versed.[2] Thus, when comparing the results of a survey taken at the beginning of the term to the results of a survey taken at the end of the term, a seemingly stagnant self-reported level of familiarity within a particular dimension would not necessarily indicate a lack of growth because the student's awareness of the scope of that skill set may have increased proportionately to his gained experience.

I decided to run the same assignment the following semester, only changing the survey proctored at the end of the course to include near-duplicate questions on each workflow: one question asking about the students' familiarity with that skill set as they felt in the moment of assessment just before the final critique, with a paired question asking how familiar they thought they had been with that same skill set when the semester began. Again, the students were never reminded of their beginning-of-semester survey responses after our initial meeting. The responses to that second survey showed strong trends of growth across the spectrum of skill sets. Many reported familiarity levels were still stagnant or somewhat lower on the spectrum compared to the answers provided at the beginning of the semester, but excitingly, responses generally showed that students were aware that they had undergone a period of growth in those areas (figure 5.1).

That was fall 2015, my most recent semester teaching a full course. The summer before, I had started working full time at the University of Texas at Arlington (UTA) Libraries' FabLab, happy to be on the leadership team steering the future developments of the small makerspace in the library that had been so meaningful for my MFA research. As it turns out, teaching upper-level studio arts courses while working a separate job forty-plus hours a week is stressful, so I have been focusing my professional energies on the FabLab ever since.

FIGURE 5.1

Illustrative set of responses from the same student in my fall 2015 Sculpture course: pre-semester survey (*left*), dual-post survey (*right*). Note the pattern of responses to the first skill set "Measuring."

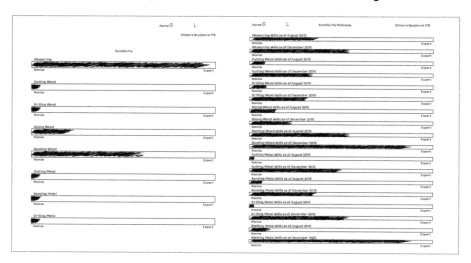

EXPANDING THE SCOPE OF THE FABLAB

One of the principle organizational goals I was hired to help bring into reality with the FabLab team was to diversify our user base from primarily male engineers to an honest plurality reflective of the campus population. Cultivating the conditions for this cultural shift primarily involved hiring student staff from diverse academic, personal, and cultural backgrounds, as well as instituting training protocol to enable FabLab staff to meet learners at their need when they came in to make.[3] Beyond that, I assigned my own class to create a project using the tools in the FabLab and encouraged other art faculty to do so with their classes. To empower art students to make effective use of technologies that their professors were as yet unaccustomed to using themselves, I worked with interested art faculty to offer in-depth tours, demonstrations, and software instruction for their classes.

Parallel to this endeavor, a few engineering faculty had been assigning students to complete projects that required the use of FabLab tools, though we had generally only been finding out about these when a flood of students would inundate the lab to make similar projects within a noticeably defined time span. I made a point of talking with these students to figure out who the professors were and to get a handle on the scope of the assignments, then reached out to the faculty to set up meetings in hopes of establishing better coordination of due dates between courses, set expectations regarding the capabilities and shortcomings of our equipment, and discuss how we might best help them achieve their intended student learning objectives.

These efforts were ongoing when the intra-Libraries, interdepartmental collaboration between the FabLab and the Experiential Learning and Outreach Department embarked on a series of events that would become the Maker Literacies program. Gretchen Trkay (department head of Experiential Learning and Outreach) had asked Katie Musick Peery (director of the UTA FabLab) and me to serve on the search committee for a science and engineering librarian, who ultimately ended up also becoming the first Maker Literacies librarian. Throughout the process of working together to determine the best person for that role, we discussed ways in which our departments ought to be working in closer concert, though I don't think any of us had in mind at the time exactly what that was going to look like or just how close we were about to become.

THE DAWN OF MAKER LITERACIES

Shortly after Martin Wallace joined UTA Libraries as the science and engineering / Maker Literacies librarian, he called for the formation of a Maker
Literacies Task Force (MLTF); I brought into the conversation two art faculty
who had been the most enthusiastic about integrating digital fabrication
technologies into their students' projects:

> **Dr. Amanda Alexander** runs the Art Education program and had also
> been one of the faculty advisors for my MFA thesis; she and I were
> already many conversations deep into the applicability of these tech-
> nologies in studio arts practice and the implications of proactively
> building opportunities for arts education students to become familiar
> with the makerspace ethos before it barged into the classrooms they
> would lead in their careers.
>
> **Gregory Scott Cook** was a new faculty member who had a wealth of expe-
> rience using digital fabrication processes in his own studio practice
> and was eager to expand the use of these tools and methodologies
> in the Art + Art History Department. Scott attended some of the task
> force meetings and was a wonderful reinforcement in our collective
> conversations regarding the pace and process of guiding students
> through the acquisition of digital fabrication skills, though he did
> not formally join the task force.

Other chapters cover the character of the task force's efforts to establish
the list of competencies (see chapter 2); I will just say here that all voices
were important—faculty and librarian alike—in coming up with a list that
encompassed the fullest spectrum of transferable skills gained in the pursuit
of making a "thing." As with all experimental endeavors, we knew that this
list was an iterative effort from the outset and that we would inevitably find
flaws once we rolled it out. Nonetheless, we put a lot of effort into our initial
attempt to create a list that was sufficiently specific to be meaningful while
remaining spacious enough to be relevant for any maker project.

Discussions I had with most faculty during the task force meetings con-
cerning curriculum tended to be along the lines of explaining the functional
capabilities of certain technologies in lay terms and consulting on potential

assignments for their classes, as I found myself situated at the functional crossroads of skill sets the task force sought to bring together. I occupied a unique space in the makeup of the group because I was the sole member of the library team who had previously been faculty in another department (though all the other librarians had experience teaching) and because my time as a graduate student was closer at hand than it was for any of my colleagues in the group. Their shared wisdom from years of professional experience offered plenty of opportunities for me to learn from them across the spectrum from conceptual to applied insights, especially regarding the ecosystem of existing competencies and literacies standards as well as patience with the facilitation of a long-term library initiative.

Certainly, the most conversed and coveted facet of my differentiation on the task force was that I was the only member of the library team, and one of only two voices in any of the task force meetings, to have anything beyond preliminary familiarity with digital fabrication tools. My own years of experience using these workflows in my studio practice and in the studio-based classroom teaching the associated skills to sculpture students gave me perspective on the range of lived experiences for those heretofore hypothetical students who would soon be assigned to make under the banner of Maker Literacies curriculum. I took seriously the sense of responsibility to ensure that everyone at the table understood the realistic capabilities of the equipment in the FabLab when conceptualizing an assignment, rather than operating from assumptions about ease of use as conveyed by too many marketing campaigns and giddily gobsmacked evangelists talking up the boundless potentials of rapid prototyping and virtual reality.

With this unique role on our team, I have organically taken lead of the Libraries' side of conversations with professors regarding pedagogical strategies for integrating the FabLab into their class(es). At times, these were group conversations in which other faculty, other librarians, or both contributed to the conversation, and at other times these were one-on-one meetings with faculty; regardless of the context in which the curriculum planning took place, it was always approached as a collaborative effort to achieve the best possible outcomes for students, faculty, makerspace staff, and librarians alike. The collaborative process with the first two art faculty was, from my perspective, as equally enjoyable between them as it was two wholly different experiences.

ART 4365: TECHNOLOGY IN ART EDUCATION

Dr. Alexander's course is a senior seminar for students in their last semester of the art education major. The students who enroll in this course are part of a cohort that has already bonded in multiple classes together as part of the degree program; all students are required to have completed their student teaching semester in the term preceding this course. In prior semesters, the technologies this course had focused on integrating were digital media for presentation of information to K–12 students in these future teachers' classrooms, such as PowerPoint and basic web design, and some of the Adobe Creative Suite as a platform they ought to be familiar with and able to teach. Initial conversations with Dr. Alexander about potential Maker Literacies projects for this class were focused on the anticipated skills gap because she had perceived in her years of leading the program that art education students did not tend to be among the early adopters of new technologies. With this observation in mind, we thought about the capabilities these students would be bringing with them, seeking ways to leverage their existing abilities to drive their interest in learning the new skills required for digital fabrication. Given that this cohort would have been fresh off their first formal experience in a functioning classroom, we decided to ask students to identify an issue they had observed in their student teaching classrooms and design a solution that could be accomplished with their novice skills in a relatively quick turnaround time.

We anticipated that students in this situation would gravitate toward simpler solutions such as downloading a Creative Commons–licensed 3D model of a mundane object like a light switch cover, perhaps modifying it with the teacher's name, and be satisfied that they had successfully engaged with new technologies. We wanted to push them farther than that while still encouraging the use of open-licensed repositories as source material for inspiration and components to be used in their designed solutions. One of the main mechanisms for prompting students to think beyond their initial ideas was to build into the assignment a requirement for them to evaluate the cost-benefit of designing and making their "thing" as compared to purchasing an existing commercially available option. Requiring students to research existing products would give them ideas about how others had attempted to solve the problems they had identified, and we hoped this exploration would naturally lead them to fabricate more custom solutions and prompt a little more out-of-the-box thinking. Some successful projects in this regard have used the example of existing products as direct inspiration, such as chair-back storage/organizers with bespoke pockets for the specific art materials used in the observed classroom. Other students have invented creative and age-appropriate physical systems to incentivize group or class behavior, keeping track of progress toward some prize while also intrinsically providing an engaging reward when learners are prompted to add markers for good performance.

We have continued to integrate this course into the FabLab every year since our initial effort, adjusting our approach each term as we learn. The primary evolution in this regard has been scheduling midpoint critiques in which I serve as subject matter expert to formally give students direct feedback about their project progress and strategies for improvement going forward. We also now schedule workdays during which the class meets in the lab a few times after the initial introduction to the space and software, rather than leaving the time-management discipline to come back anytime the lab is open entirely to the students.

ART 4392: EMERGING TECHNOLOGIES

The curriculum analysis process with Scott Cook was entirely different from the preceding art education process because the whole premise of his course was to introduce students to digital fabrication tools and workflows. This was the only studio arts class included in the initial set of pilot courses, and even among studio arts classes it was a distinct outlier in that the students would already be making use of the technologies we support in the FabLab as an inherent part of their assignments. This factor made for an interesting series of discussions between Scott and myself and within the Maker Literacies Task Force (MLTF). It was obvious that Scott's perspective within the MLTF conversations had been particularly valuable, but it was perhaps less clear that this specific course would fit within the ethos of what the Maker Literacies initiative set out to achieve. We were thus at a crossroads where we needed to delineate the primary goal of the Maker Literacies program under the conditions of a new lens; up to that point, the integration of hands-on making experiences (mostly utilizing the lowered skills-threshold for achieving high-quality outputs as afforded by digital fabrication tools) into classrooms and curricula that would otherwise have no engagement with the technologies had been a central focus of our efforts, but was it the guiding principle?

We determined that because the competencies had been established with the intent to outline higher-level learning outcomes and transferable skills associated with making, the core of our program was not the *introduction* of digital fabrication (as was the case in every other pilot course) but the *assessment* of experiential learning assignments within the hybrid realm of the makerspace classroom. We had been intentional in our crafting of the beta competencies to remain largely technology agnostic, though this goal had initially been more concerned with avoiding obsolescence as technologies evolved. Through these conversations, we also came to consensus that we did want participation in the Maker Literacies program to involve some shift in curricular approach from whatever had been initially planned for the course. In this case, we felt that assessing the students on their familiarity with the act of making might not be especially meaningful as a part of our program; Maker Literacies is more than a platform for assessment of studio arts education.

Re-viewing our beta list of competencies in this new light guided us to conceptualize an assignment which would mandate that the students share the knowledge they had gained throughout the semester in workshops that were open to the public and hosted in the Central Library (either in the FabLab itself or in a computer lab for software instruction). Students were required to work in teams to prepare materials and lesson plans that would guide an audience having unknown or mixed skill levels through their chosen process. This exercise in knowledge management required students to think more systematically about software and processes they had learned from functionalist perspectives; many reported that they had never seen themselves as knowledgeable enough to teach others and that this assignment challenged them to both learn the skills more thoroughly and trust their ability to help others learn.

The workshops also presented an opportunity for us to manifest a mantra Scott had been repeating throughout several of our meetings and conversations—that he wanted his students to be "ambassadors for the FabLab." In the early contexts of our discussions, the assertion was generally that students would make interesting projects using the tools in the FabLab, show those projects to their friends and classmates, and thus generate interest among other students to use the FabLab themselves. The workshops were a way to evolve this notion into an integrated function of the class that both directly put his students into that ambassadorial role and created student-led events in our student-centric space.

AMBASSADOR FOR STUDIO ARTS EDUCATION

Throughout the MLTF meetings, especially when brainstorming potential projects and curricular concepts with faculty, I kept coming back to the notion of studio arts education as a precedent for the types of pedagogy we were trying to encourage. Although the zeitgeist of makerspaces didn't arise until the past decade or so, there have been designated spaces within human societies for making all manner of things since time immemorial. The question of the extent to which these skilled-craft workshops, laboratories, and arts studios might be considered proto-makerspaces is an ongoing conversation beyond the scope of this chapter. What is important in this context is that many contemporary makerspaces notably differ from the tradition of spaces for making things in that maker culture overtly celebrates interdisciplinary approaches to solving problems through the iterative process.

This earnest embrace of interdisciplinarity recognizes the varied values, approaches, and skill sets of makers seeking to self-actualize away from passive consumerism and has been the leading cultural commonality defining the maker movement. Tools are important, though solely focusing on providing access to equipment is an entirely different goal than cultivating a community of mutual empowerment based on interdisciplinary admiration and nimble mental modalities. For far longer than the maker movement has existed as a definable phenomenon, the contemporary arts world has been abuzz with cross-pollination between scientific themes in content and the exploration of technology through and as material; artists' respect for scientists, mathematicians, and engineers—and the contributions they make to society through technological (and theoretical) innovation—is widespread. In spite of the individual scientists who appreciate the arts and hold artists in high esteem, this respect often does not feel reciprocal within the halls of academia. Smart students are habitually discouraged from scholarly pursuit of their passions within the arts out of a supposed concern for practicality, notwithstanding the fact that the training in creative thinking that is at the core of any quality education in the arts becomes a suite of lifelong transferable skills which remain applicable throughout unpredictable shifts in job markets.

The dawning recognition that creativity is not only crucial to all fields of inquiry but must be actively cultivated through the intentional design of the learning environment in which students interact while they are building their understandings of the world is steadily spreading beyond the more commonly constructivist context of early childhood education. The comprehension of phenomena intended to be taught through the study of science, technology, engineering, and mathematics too often stays trapped in the theoretical realm, and even students who seem to excel in the classroom find themselves struggling with basic application of those concepts in the real world. Curriculum is not just made more interesting via hands-on projects; such engagement beyond the textbook is essential to allow students to experience abstract concepts using other senses and modalities of thought.

Crucially, these lessons ought to be imbued with an open-ended spirit that embraces multiple potential outcomes (within the boundaries of safety concerns), with project parameters designed to require students to flex multiple skill sets simultaneously. This experiential complement to traditional academic study is necessary not because art is fun and play is important but because the creative engagement of the mind reinforces theoretical studies in a fundamentally different way that procedural labs cannot. When all these concerns combine, the supposedly stark separation between teaching strategies in STEM and academic art diffuses into a spectrum of similarities. Rather than considering theories and principles in isolation, true STEAM pedagogy dovetails perfectly with the ethos of the maker movement, meeting challenges with a holistic approach that recognizes the scaffolded and faceted nature of every project; there are always other perspectives to consider, rabbit holes of information to explore and digest, more techniques to learn and practice. The core life skills learned through making are the abilities to determine the relevant aspects to consider within an open framework, draw on one's life experiences to implement existing transferable skills and identify areas of ignorance, learn the missing links while leaving most yaks unshorn, and iterate through failures toward a refined result.

Rapid prototyping and digital fabrication tools can obviously help with this design cycle, though the community of support and the cultivation of interdisciplinary thought patterns are far more important than access to any particular tool. In my visits to other academic makerspaces, I hear a lot of recognition of this truism even as we all pack as many tools and technologies into our spaces as budgets allow. Unfortunately, I have also noticed a pattern of rebranding traditional fabrication labs and machine shops as "makerspaces" despite a continued adherence to the traditions of curricular prerequisites for accessing the tools and an inflexibility on the part of the managers of such spaces that expects students to come to them already conforming to best practices for workflows they have never gone through before. Additionally, there is a troubling theme within some academic makerspaces and makerspace curriculum initiatives of effectively employing the diversified pedagogy of STEAM in practice without recognition by name; the co-option of the makerspace movement by proponents of STEM education seems to miss the point. STEM education has emphasized the primacy of rote digestion of theoretical concepts and placed such central value on the ability to memorize equations that the performance of that recall on demand served as a functional prerequisite for actually building anything. How many consecutive semesters of success in a read-and-regurgitate model did engineering undergraduates need before they were trusted enough to gain any access to departmental lab spaces? Perhaps more importantly, how much better would those same students have performed in their traditional coursework if they had simultaneous access to lab spaces that were specifically intended for experiential experimentation?

Artists and art educators, on the other hand, have long since jettisoned the model of rote copying of the masters and are instead staunch advocates for access to tools and the opportunity to use them to explore concepts early in one's education because the value of making things for oneself is almost always far more important than the object being made. The art studio is inherently a platform for experiential learning.[4] Hands-on making helps us understand materials and processes in a visceral way that a mathematical formula simply cannot, just as defining something mathematically helps identify patterns that might otherwise elude one's internalized sensibilities. The embrace of iterative design—working through the inescapability of failures as one seeks slippery successes—is suffused in both arts education and makerspace culture; as iterative design, experiential learning, and creative thinking are increasingly emphasized in the study of all disciplines, let us collectively abandon the stale silos that have confined the way we conceptualize subject matter pedagogy.

Science, Technology, Engineering, and Mathematics are undeniably crucial to our society; it does not minimize their importance in the slightest to formally recognize the significance of Art to any society, just as recognizing the educational value of Art pedagogy does not diminish the educational value of Science, Technology, Engineering, and Mathematics as important subjects for all students to study. Indeed, maintaining an artificial divide between STEM and the Arts forces students to think of themselves (and others) in tribalist "two-culture" terms, constraining our ability to cultivate well-rounded members of society.[5] It feels somewhat disingenuous and unnecessarily divisive to ignore the relationship between the type of learning that happens in makerspaces (which is now being recognized to be a viable pedagogical strategy for all disciplines of inquiry) and the studio-based experiential learning model that has long been integral to arts education. We are stronger together; makerspaces are constructivist platforms for STEAM education.

The Maker Literacies initiative was not at all intended as an experiment to prove this point. In the process of collaborating on curriculum design with professors, however, I've come to realize that many of my suggestions are essentially studio arts projects rooted in the course content of other departments. When we integrate the FabLab into a class that would not normally be making, we are not just introducing those students to technologies, we are familiarizing them with a powerful way of thinking to which they have been underexposed; by assessing their growth within this context, we are establishing a record of how studio-based pedagogical patterns enhance the intended student learning outcomes across disciplines.

FLYING BEYOND PILOTS

Before our work to establish Maker Literacies assessment techniques, our interactions with students and faculty had been similar to what countless others in academic makerspaces had been experiencing: obviously meaningful experiences for students that yielded interesting anecdotes without much in terms of comparable results. One of the central ambitions of the Maker Literacies initiative has been to bridge this gap by providing an assessment structure that is easily applicable to a wide variety of course types. Ultimately, this goal has meant creating a uniform format for feedback about transdisciplinary learning while mindfully avoiding the turbulent current of standardized knowledge assessment.

After the first year of running pilot courses, it became clear to Martin, Gretchen, Katie, and myself that the disparate styles of faculty-determined assessment feedback we were receiving from each class were insufficient to provide comparable results between classes; we needed to standardize our assessment strategy, not just the competencies being assessed. We determined that we could write questions based on each competency and that Likert-scale responses would provide the most stable platform for all course types to provide student self-assessment data. It was at this point that I shared my experience with assessing my sculpture students, discussed at the beginning of this chapter. I had been quite interested in the further investigation of the dual-post strategy (asking students at the end of the term to reflect on their perception of growth by providing two separate answers for each competency question in the post-project survey), though I had not had the opportunity to pursue this interest after I stopped teaching classes. Following some discussion among the four of us, we decided to test the applicability of the dual-post survey structure to our new beta surveys.

As we internally evolved our approach to assessment in preparation for the first Institute of Museum and Library Services (IMLS) grant, we also made steady progress in involving more faculty at UTA each semester. The various responsibilities of the four librarians working on this project increasingly led Martin and me to conduct the day-to-day work within the initiative, with Martin taking lead on the assessment administration while I took lead on developing curriculum with faculty and teaching instructional sessions for each class.

The following selection of courses provides a series of illustrative windows into processes that played out in the curriculum development for all the Maker Literacies classes.

IE 4340: Engineering Project Management

Dr. Jaime Cantu has been enthusiastically involved with Maker Literacies for several semesters (see chapter 6); from the outset of discussing potential projects that his course could be based on, he was excited about the prospect of ensuring that his students were required to use as many different technologies in the FabLab as we could feasibly facilitate. The collaborative process of figuring out what somewhat-standardized object could be produced that would reasonably incorporate equipment from all across the lab was a fun exercise in project ideation. Beyond the embellished dress shirts and subsequent sewn horses, however, the issue of assessing his chosen competency of teamwork among group members required a creative work-around due to our collective oversight on the MLTF when establishing the list of beta competencies: we had enumerated a competency about forming meaningful teams but had not noticed that we omitted any competencies about working effectively with teammates! We considered revising the beta list to amend this omission but were reticent to do so because we knew we would be finding many issues we would want to change as we worked through applying the system to class assessment, and we thought it would be best to save all those changes for the officially revised version rather than confusing everyone involved with a multitude of beta lists.

In a meeting with Dr. Cantu, Martin, Katie, and myself, we were discussing what to do about this issue when I realized that we had a hidden solution built in to our surveys already: at the beginning of the semester, students in all participating classes self-assess their skills with each piece of equipment in the FabLab as well as whichever competencies have been selected with faculty. I floated the idea to the group that we could provide anonymized results of that initial assessment to Dr. Cantu and have the students go through an exercise to decide how to build their teams based on the data (without knowing which of their classmates are being grouped together). Dr. Cantu then would send the grouped anonymized identifiers to us, we'd decode the list, and send him the groups by student name. This process also preserved the integrity of our research protocol in that the faculty member would not be able to see students' responses, avoiding any potentially improper influence on grading. This team-building exercise has been of interest to several faculty, and we continue to use this method in multiple classes.

EDML 4372: Mathematics in the Middle Grades

Dr. Christopher Kribs was introduced to our Maker Literacies research through faculty outreach events conducted by UTA Libraries and wanted to involve his class that prepares future middle school math teachers. Many of his students are commuter students who are already involved in their student teaching work and are thus stretched rather thin in their capacity to take on additional time commitments. Dr. Kribs had wanted to introduce his students to 3D printing by having them all print the same file downloaded from Thingiverse in their chosen color and then do an exercise in class to calculate the volume of the object. I was not enthusiastic about including a class with a project like this in our study because it seemed minimally engaging for students and ignored several accessible software tools that could easily enhance the experientiality of the lesson. It felt especially important to design engaging curriculum for a class of future teachers in order to better prepare them in turn to design more robust learning experiences for their future middle school math students.

Dr. Kribs and I met several times, going over his intended student learning outcomes for the course and familiarizing him with the equipment in the FabLab and the software used to prepare files. We discussed the volume calculation feature commonly built in to 3D modeling software and how the existence of such a tool might be used to push student exploration of volumetric calculations to gain a better understanding of the relative volumes of different shapes without having to do the calculations longhand. I also introduced him to Tinkercad, a 3D modeling software that we suggest learners start with if they do not have existing modeling skills. We worked through a few designs in Tinkercad, and once he saw the capability of the software, realized how approachable it is, and had some time to explore it on his own, we reconvened to decide how to move forward with his class. It was an ideal collaborative brainstorm: we both came to the table with ideas that the other riffed on and in the back-and-forth came to a really exciting project based on creating manipulatives. Commercially available manipulatives are almost all set up to illustrate the logic of decimals, giving physical form to our familiar base-10 system. What if, we wondered together, we taught the students how to 3D model and had them design manipulatives that would illustrate alternate base systems or fractions, or both, beyond the common division by twos?

We ran this assignment in Dr. Kribs's class multiple times with great success. The next step, which we have not had the opportunity to enact and assess yet, is to measure the effectiveness of the custom manipulatives in the real-life classrooms where young students are trying to learn the concepts these educational tools are intended to demonstrate.

HIST 4332: History of the Book

Dr. Kathryne Beebe designed her History of the Book course around a capti-vating question: "How do changes in the technologies of writing and reading affect the way we think?" In my first year working in the library, I had seen a poster for this class and contacted the professor out of sheer interest; our conversations led to my serving as an embedded mentor for the class. A couple of years later, with Maker Literacies under way and the FabLab significantly more established, Dr. Beebe taught the class again, and we integrated the History of the Book with an optional final project made in the makerspace instead of a traditional term paper. Students who chose the maker term proj-ect were prompted to create a cultural artifact that meaningfully engaged with some aspect(s) of the technological and conceptual changes in literate life. To prepare these history majors for this studio arts project, in which they would be trying to capture a complex of concepts gained in their research within a made object, I led instructional sessions on 3D modeling, the use of Adobe Illustrator for preparing CNC-ready files, and our new papermaking area, as well as a lesson on the use of scanned artifacts to explore digital humanities potentials.

Most of our other classes had a far more defined scope for the assigned project. The relative openness of the History of the Book assignment encour-aged students to flex their own creativity, though it also presented a problem in terms of how to structure the introductory experience. With so many tools available and potentially relevant to the students' research, and only a couple of class periods available to familiarize them with all the hardware and soft-ware, I employed what I have come to think of as the "fire hose" approach: introductions to the equipment, broad explanations of how the tools work, explanations of how to prepare files, demonstrations of the tools in action, and examples of completed projects are presented in sequence and at a pace that allows for questions but is definitely too rapid to expect the uninitiated to absorb all the information. Before embarking on this type of session, I make clear to learners that they don't need to stress about trying to memorize everything covered because they are welcome to come back during any of the ninety-plus hours a week the FabLab is open and ask further questions about anything that catches their interest during the tour. Our student staff are trained to help any learner who comes in "make just about anything," and I underscore at several points of a fire hose session that we are a teaching lab that exists to help them learn how to make whatever they want to make. In the years of seeing a sea of overwhelmed expressions on students' faces and experimenting with techniques for overcoming their understandable sense of intimidation, I've found it truly helps everyone involved if I am explicit in reiterating that *they won't be bothering us* by asking for assistance at any stage of their project: whether it be ideation, initial sketches, translating sketches to CAD, cleaning up CAD files to be CAM-ready, or machine operation—we are here to help.

SPAN 3311: Spanish Culture and Civilization

Dr. Amy Austin teaches a Spanish Culture and Civilization course in the Modern Languages Department as a historical survey of the Iberian Peninsula and an examination of how the cultural conflicts of the past continue to inform contemporary culture in Spain. Because it is a language class, all the readings and all the class discussions are conducted in Spanish. As someone who was a German major for a couple of years at the beginning of my undergraduate studies, I know the importance of immersive experiences to the language learning process. In a meeting with Dr. Austin and Martin, I pitched an idea with plenty of qualifiers about whether it would be possible, but if Dr. Austin were interested, I would pursue it: some of our FabLab student employees are bilingual, and we could potentially conduct the tour *todos en español.*

Dr. Austin was thrilled with the prospect, so I identified the Spanish-speaking student employees whose schedule availability aligned with the course meeting time and worked with them to develop their tour-giving abilities and ensure that they had time to familiarize themselves with the technical terms they might not be used to using with their families (reminding them that the students in the class probably wouldn't be familiar with those terms either, so it would definitely help if the staff members explained some of the technical words as they were introduced).

Structurally, this class assignment is rather similar to that for the History of the Book, except that Dr. Austin does not give students the option of writing a traditional term paper; all students in the class make a cultural artifact using FabLab tools to respond to some of the major controversies in the history of the Iberian Peninsula. The wide-open possibilities for selecting materials and equipment created a scenario in which the fire hose session would be employed, and I discussed my concerns about this approach with Dr. Austin before our initial attempt. The fire hose of information can be a lot for any student to process, especially one unfamiliar with foundational design skills; we had a fairly strong sense that very few, if any, of these students would be coming into the class with any background in design. In addition, I questioned whether the linguistic factor in this class and the fact that student staff would be leading the session (because my Spanish-language abilities are nowhere near enough to pull this off) would be too many variables to guarantee students' success in the project.

We discussed potential approaches, and after checking her course outline, Dr. Austin determined that because she wanted to make this project a requirement worth a significant portion of the students' final grade, she could dedicate additional class meetings as workdays to follow up in the FabLab to ensure that students were making progress and getting the feedback they needed.

Ultimately, FabLab staff led four eighty-minute class sessions—a tour, software instruction, and two workdays in the makerspace—and we attended the final presentations at the end of the semester. This commitment of time and preparatory energy by both faculty and library staff is certainly not a scalable model to employ with every integrated class, but it catapulted these students into making some of the strongest projects any class has made in our years of FabLab curricular integrations. We have now run this class three times and have started encouraging selected humanities classes and others outside the traditional making domains to schedule mediated workdays for their students in the lab because the positive impact of these constructively critical interventions on the quality of student output is undeniable.

CONCLUSION

There exists a certain circularity to the disambiguation of how the arts courses we have partnered with have influenced the development of the Maker Literacies program and thus the classes from other disciplines, or how my perspectives as an ambassador for studio arts education have shaped our program based on what I bring to the table. As someone with an uncommonly diverse educational history, I see myself fulfilling a translational role facilitating a more holistic framing that takes intended student learning outcomes, curricular constructs, technological tools, and oft-competing value systems between disciplines into consideration to find the commonalities and resultant opportunities for hybridization. My perspectives on pedagogy were forged throughout a lifetime of interest in the art of teaching, and my practical experience of teaching has primarily been in studio arts classrooms; the experimental nature of our experiential learning curriculum development has provided opportunities to test and ultimately reinforce my sense of the validity of studio arts strategies in other disciplinary contexts.

This work will never feel complete; there will always be lessons gleaned from the frustrations and elations of prior semesters to tune our approaches going forward, as well as new classes and different professors to collaborate with. At times, I miss being a professor with my own curriculum and set of students to guide through a semester on their individual paths to mastery, though I feel outstandingly fortunate to be situated where I am now. My role in the FabLab, especially within the Maker Literacies initiative, has afforded me the opportunity to engage in some degree of mentorship with exponentially more students than I could ever hope to accomplish without the collaborative efforts of so many skilled and passionate colleagues.

NOTES

1. Sonia L. J. White, Linda J. Graham, and Sabrina Blass, "Why Do We Know So Little about the Factors Associated with Gifted Underachievement? A Systematic Literature Review," *Educational Research Review* 24 (2018): 55–66.

2. Justin Kruger and David Dunning, "Unskilled and Unaware of It: How Difficulties in Recognizing One's Own Incompetence Lead to Inflated Self-Assessments," *Journal of Personality and Social Psychology* 77, no. 6 (1999): 1121–34.

3. Katie Musick Peery and Morgan Chivers, "Diversity by Design: How to Create and Sustain an Inclusive Academic Library Makerspace," in *Re-Making the Library Makerspace: Critical Theories, Reflections, and Practices*, edited by Maggie Melo and Jennifer Nichols (Sacramento, CA: Library Juice Press, forthcoming).

4. Richard Lachapelle, "Experiential Learning and Discipline-Based Art Education," *Visual Arts Research* 23, no. 2 (1997): 135–44.

5. Gregory McNamee, "Erasing the Gap between Art and Science," *Science Magazine—Careers,* May 2001, https://www.sciencemag.org/careers/2001/05/erasing-gap -between-art-and-science.

Design and Implementation in a Project Management Course

Jaime Cantu

Experience teaches nothing. In fact there is no experience to record without theory. . . . Without theory there is no learning . . . . And that is their downfall. People copy examples and then they wonder what is the trouble. They look at examples and without theory they learn nothing.

—W. EDWARDS DEMING[1]

The preceding quotation from Deming has stuck with me since I came across it during graduate school. My first foray into industry was as a manufacturing engineer, and a key skill in production and inventory control is scheduling. Yet, with my background in computer engineering, I had no idea where to start. I often found myself looking at historical data and asking my supervisors and colleagues for advice. I was essentially copying examples with no theoretical background.

When I went to graduate school for my MS in systems and engineering management, I finally learned the theory, and it all came together.

As a professor, I found myself reflecting on Deming's words once again when a senior mechanical engineering student in my project management (PM) class said, "I was iffy on this class in the beginning, but I really wish I had taken this class three years ago." Engineering Project Management at the University of Texas at Arlington (UTA) is a senior-level engineering course required for industrial engineering (IE) but elective for other engineering majors. The class is commonly made up of industrial, mechanical, and electrical engineers. When I started asking students when their particular majors introduced PM tools, I was often told it was during design labs when professors asked them to create Gantt charts, work breakdown schedule (WBS) milestones, and requirement documents. The students then complied by looking for examples of these PM tools and copying them. In their self-assessment survey responses at the start of the PM course, students express confidence about their experience with PM tools and believe they can use the tools effectively. Yet, at the end of the semester after learning the theory and applying PM tools in the FabLab, students report that they initially did not have a comprehensive understanding.

PM certificates are managed by such organizations as the Project Management Institute (PMI) or the American Society for Engineering Management (ASEM). These organizations offer books, certifications, and study guides for learning the various PM tools. Review workshops are available to help individuals prepare for such certifications as Project Management Professional (PMP); this approach makes sense for working professionals. People gain experience in industry, learn the theory, and, after so many hours, sit for a certification exam. So, the question is, how do we replicate this experience at the undergraduate level? Currently, many lab courses claim they will introduce students to PM but rarely provide the time during the semester to do so. Allowing students to learn theory and gain experience during a one-semester course is difficult. One way to alleviate this difficulty is to incorporate makerspaces into the curriculum. The UTA FabLab allows students to use the theory learned in PM to create an interdisciplinary team, design a product, and implement it within one semester. Along the way we are developing metrics to measure the effectiveness of the implementations to better develop lessons based on experiential learning.

The purpose of the Engineering Project Management course is to expose undergraduates to creating teams, using PM tools, and working on a project using the FabLab in the library. Students receive a tour of the FabLab before the assignment of the project and then create teams using the data provided from a survey that assesses each individual's skill levels (see chapter 5). The project phases consist of idea, design, prototype, and production of a semester project. After students create teams for the class project, they meet with their teams and present ideas and designs for the first two phases. A subject matter expert (SME) from the FabLab attends the presentations and judges the feasibility of the ideas given the equipment currently available. Several weeks later, the teams present their prototypes and discuss what issues arose and what actions are to be taken before final production. At the final production phase, the teams must display a functional product. This chapter will first provide a brief background about PM tools and theories and then discuss methods and results, focusing on pre- and post-surveys, the interdisciplinary team design, team evaluation design, and how to incorporate the FabLab throughout the semester.

In many ways, engineering departments were some of the original makers. During my sophomore year as an electrical engineering undergraduate, we were assigned a spot in the basement lab where we could check out equipment to complete the various semester projects assigned. One of the first things I did was disassemble a wireless phone to see if I could trace the circuitry. I also used an oscilloscope to figure out how remote-controlled cars received signals. All this led to my receiving a C in my project lab, probably because these projects weren't the ones assigned to me! I believe this ability to pursue my innate curiosity about the world led me to learn a lot and, eventually, to receive my PhD in engineering. The maker movement isn't new, but the idea of making equipment easily available to the whole student population is fresh and exciting. No longer do you have to be an engineering major to have access to a particular piece of equipment.

PROJECT MANAGEMENT AND THE STAGE-GATE PROCESS

Management is a process concerned with the achievement of goals or objectives. Project management involves the coordination of group activity wherein the manager plans, organizes, staffs, directs, and controls to achieve an objective with constraints on time, cost, and performance of the end product. Planning is the process of preparing for the commitment of resources in the most effective fashion. Controlling is the process of making events conform to schedules by coordinating the action of all parts of the organization according to the plan established for attaining the objective. As project managers assess their resources, materials, equipment, and facilities, they must consider time, cost, and quality as the big three items not only in the selection but also in the management of all resources throughout the project life cycle. This focus ensures that a project is completed on schedule and on budget and meets the customer's expectations of quality. An important aspect of managing time, cost, and quality for project work activities is the interconnection of these three elements. Any change to one of these elements has an effect on one or both of the others, which introduces constraints the project manager must handle. This concept is known as the *triple constraint.*[2]

The project manager is responsible for coordinating and integrating activities across multiple functional lines. Integration activities include activities necessary to develop a project plan, activities necessary to execute the plan, and activities necessary to make changes to the plan. A project manager must convert resources into outputs, services, and, ultimately, profits. For this to happen, the project manager needs strong communicative and interpersonal skills, must become familiar with the operation, and must know about the technology being used. Essentially, the project manager is a general manager and gets to know the total operations of the company.[3]

When companies recognize the need to begin developing processes for project management, the starting point is normally the stage-gate process. The stage-gate process was created because the traditional organizational structure was designed primarily for top-down, centralized management, control, and communications, all of which were no longer practical for organizations that use project management and horizontal workflow. Stages are groups of activities that can be performed either in series or parallel based upon the magnitude of the risks the project team can endure. The gates are structured decision points at the end of each stage; good project management processes usually have no more than six gates. With more than six gates, the project team focuses too much attention on preparing for the gate reviews rather than on the actual management of the project.

Project managers are never allowed to function as their own gatekeepers. The gatekeepers are either individuals or groups of individuals designated by senior management and empowered to enforce the structured decision-making process. The gatekeepers are authorized to evaluate performance to date against predetermined criteria and to provide the project team with additional business and technical information. The stage-gate process is neither an end result nor a self-sufficient methodology. Because the stage-gate process focuses on decision-making more than on life-cycle phases, the stage-gate process is being used as an internal, decision-making tool within each of the life-cycle phases. The advantage is that, though life-cycle phases are the same for every project, the stage-gate process can be custom-designed for each project to facilitate decision-making and risk management.

SEMESTER PROJECT

My Engineering Project Management course introduces project management (PM) concepts and tools needed to form, develop, and manage cross-disciplinary engineering design teams. Overarching topics include understanding research and development (R&D) organizations, teams and work groups, job design specifications, organizational effectiveness, and how to lead technical professionals. Students complete a team-based, semester-long project to gain hands-on experience with PM tools, techniques, and principles, including project planning (requirement specifications, statement of work, and work breakdown schedule), network scheduling techniques (program evaluation and review technique, critical path method), project graphics (Gantt charts, etc.), pricing and estimating (effort-hours/task/job code, overhead and fringe rate), risk management, and performance appraisals (tracking team member performance, providing feedback, resolving issues).

During the semester, the class proceeds through four stages: concept, design, prototype, and final product. Initially, I divided the stages equally over the semester, but several issues arose, so the final time frame provides two weeks for the concept stage, two weeks for design, three weeks for the prototype stage, and five weeks for the final product stage. The most important factors leading to this time frame were the need to train students on FabLab equipment and the need to provide enough time after the prototype phase for students to fix the inevitable issues with their initial ideas. Each stage ends with a presentation and documents assigned for that particular stage.

The specific semester project that I assign this class changes yearly. The examples and data in this chapter are from two iterations of this project: the "Mini Mav" and the "Mav Shirt." The Mini Mav is a stuffed horse or unicorn based on the Vogue V9194 pattern, and the Mav Dress Shirt is based on McCall's M6932 sewing pattern. The overarching methods for assessing the semester-long project included a project rubric, an oral progress presentation at midterm with open Q&A, and a final oral presentation with open Q&A. Teams showcased their completed products during their final oral presentation. This being a PM course and not a design course, the teams' final products were not assessed for quality, function, or aesthetics. Rather, teams were assessed for their ability to work as a team to complete the project on time while addressing all project requirements. Assembling effective teams and demonstrating understanding of digital fabrication processes, including both additive and subtractive fabrication, were two of the Maker Literacies criteria that were assessed in addition to the myriad other PM fundamentals taught in the course such as scheduling, time management, communication, cost estimation, and risk management.

Concept Phase (Brainstorming)

During the first week, students take a pre-survey asking them questions about their experiences with the FabLab equipment assigned for the upcoming project and with project management. The survey answers are imported into Excel with the student names removed and "employee numbers" assigned. The students then receive the assigned project requirements for the semester, including what the students are responsible for delivering along with which equipment in the FabLab will be used. Requirements can range from specific to vague—for example (from the Mini Mav assignment):

Team Logo: Teams will design a unique logo to represent their team. The logo will be embroidered on either the saddle, the blanket, or an accessory. The FabLab embroidery machine must be used.

Accessories: Teams will design and craft wooden accessories (surprise me!) using the FabLab.

Embellishment: Teams may embellish their Maverick or accessories or both with UTA pride for up to 3 percent extra credit. Embellishment must be part of the process and approved by Dr. Cantu.

A homework assignment tasks students to design teams using the data from the surveys, lectures from class, and project requirements. Each student designs two types of teams: a "dream team" composed of the employees whom the student believes would be the best to complete the project, and a team that "spreads the awesomeness," breaking the entire class into evenly balanced teams to complete the project. These two scenarios allow me to hone in on what the students believe will allow them to complete the project in a timely manner with adequate quality. My experience is that asking the students to answer just one of these questions doesn't work well. If asked to create teams from the entire class, they just break the class on easily divisible numbers (thirty-six students in the class equals six teams of six), or, in the dream team scenario, they will make the whole class a team, and if the names are on the data, they create a team with all their friends. I have found that asking both questions allows me to elicit a good idea of what the students feel they need to complete the project.

After the students have submitted the homework, I review the assignment and develop a consensus of what the students feel are the best team designs. I exercise instructor prerogative on the more creative or borderline solutions. Many times, students suggest ideas that sound good but are not feasible; other times, students who don't enjoy teamwork suggest a three-person team. The problem with small teams is that a student inevitably drops the course, and the team then struggles to meet deadlines and deliver the final product. In my experience, a minimum of four and a maximum of six students are needed per team for the size of projects assigned in this class; having six or more team members allows for too much slack, and students start to argue that members are not pulling their weight, given the lack of work. After reviewing the feasible solutions students have suggested, I put together teams that best match student consensus.

Teams then have two weeks to develop a concept for each requirement, along with a rough draft of RACI (Responsible, Accountable, Consulted, and Informed: roles and responsibilities for each team member per task) charts, statement of work (SOW), and peer evaluation design. A panel of subject matter experts (SMEs), consisting of library and FabLab personnel and Industrial, Manufacturing, and Systems Engineering (IMSE) faculty, is present at the concept stage gate presentation. The SMEs offer feedback on student concepts with regard to cost, feasibility, and potential problems the students may face. Figures 6.1, 6.2, and 6.3 show initial drawings and pictures of ideas that teams used to meet the requirements for the Mav Shirt and Mini Mav assignments.

FIGURE 6.1

Proposed Mav Shirt team logo design

FIGURE 6.2

Proposed Mini Mav stable concept

Design Phase

The teams have two weeks after meeting with the SMEs to finalize their designs and present at the design stage gate. Teams develop a WBS, finalize the SOW, finalize the peer evaluations for teammates, and submit milestones for which they will be held accountable. A key requirement for the teams before presenting their designs is to have started the training needed for the FabLab. Students' design expectations are more realistic after receiving feedback from FabLab staff and attending training for equipment. Figures 6.4, 6.5, and 6.6 show the final designs after meeting with the SMEs and incorporating feedback received. Feedback for the logo (see figure 6.1) consisted of removing 3D effects from the drawing because these don't translate well when embroidered. The stable diorama (see figure 6.2) was simplified, and the podium (see figure 6.3) was expanded to include backlight effects.

FIGURE 6.3

Proposed Mini Mav podium design

FIGURE 6.4

Final Mav Shirt team logo design

FIGURE 6.5

Final Mini Mav stable design

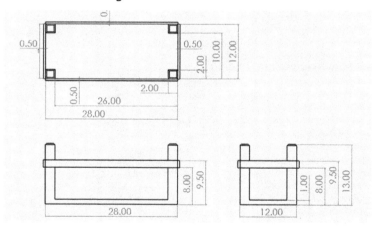

FIGURE 6.6

Final Mini Mav podium design

Prototype Phase

At the beginning of the prototype phase, I introduce a change management system. In industry, changes will occur, but it is important to document those changes. Project managers are responsible for submitting a change request form should the team deviate from the proposed design. I then review the design and decide if I will approve and respond to the request. Teams have three weeks to deliver a prototype of each requirement; they don't have to have the project assembled, but they must have done all trainings, purchased all materials, and attempted an initial trial run. I have found the prototype phase to be a key learning tool for engineering students. Many times, team members work on their individual tasks without much interaction besides progress reports. Slight variations inevitably occur, which can lead to interesting learning opportunities.

For example, one team was having trouble getting the screen print ink to dry on the initial material, so the team members responsible for the process changed to a more absorbent material. This change makes perfect sense and is a good solution, but the absorbent material was also more elastic than the original fabric, which led to a thicker and wider horse when stuffed. None of this was communicated to the team members designing the horse chute, which led to an interesting final product when fitting the horse in the chute. My goal for the prototype phase is for students to get into the habit of finding these errors, rapidly prototyping, and communicating with each other to fix any errors for the final product.

The documents for the prototype phase consist of a Gantt chart, a slack/float analysis, a PERT (Program Evaluation and Review Technique) analysis, and evaluations for all team members. At this point in the semester, students are discovering the old axiom about "best-laid plans," so I cover how to project plan in a deterministic and probabilistic way. We review the critical path method with slack/float calculations to show students that finding the critical path and managing it is key to project management. We then move on to PERT, a probabilistic model for calculating critical paths, and how to create and interpret the data. At the presentation, teams show prototypes for all project requirements, then show the deterministic models of their project, and, finally, after explaining why they are not on schedule, use PERT to give probabilities of getting back on schedule.

Final Product Phase

At the final presentation a week before finals, all SMEs are present to see whether and how their advice was taken into account. Students present from concept phase to final phase for the project along with costs. Figure 6.7 shows a final product presented for the Mav Shirt; one can see how the embroidery and wooden hanger embellishment turned out. Figure 6.8 shows how the team with the Mini Mav diorama design in figure 6.2 had to scale back their initial concept because of time constraints. The final product for the Mini Mav podium is shown in figure 6.9; the wooden stage with embellishment worked out as planned, but the screen print on the blanket was difficult to see. Both Mini Mav teams scored well through the stage-gate process but still had a few flaws with the final product. Over the semester, the students learned that documenting procedures and communication can lead to fewer errors in the final product, but that nothing is flawless. Teams then take questions from the SMEs and the audience and offer feedback to FabLab staff about what could have made their work processes easier. After the last of the presentations, I assign the post-survey.

FIGURE 6.7

Mav Shirt final product

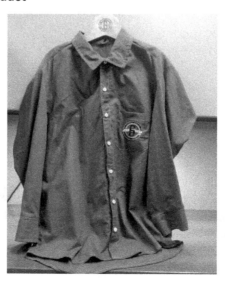

FIGURE 6.8

Mini Mav stable final product

FIGURE 6.9

Mini Mav podium final product

ASSESSMENT METRICS

As discussed earlier in this book, an initial (beta) list of eleven transdisciplinary makerspace competencies, each with multiple dimensions, was employed to measure the learning that takes place when students engage in making (appendix A). Although nearly all eleven beta makerspace competencies were highly relevant to this senior-level Engineering Project Management course, we chose to examine only two for the sake of managing our scope: "Assembles effective teams" (beta competency 4) and "Demonstrates understanding of digital fabrication process" (beta competency 8). At the time of our initial consultation for planning this course, the other, perhaps more obvious choices, such as "Applies design praxis" (beta competency 2) and "Demonstrates time management best practices" (beta competency 3), were already being implemented in numerous other courses. Neither competency 4 nor 8 had yet been adopted, so the Engineering Project Management course presented an opportunity to implement and begin collecting data about them.

Homework-based interventions for both competencies were designed and integrated into the semester-long makerspace project. Both homework assignments and the overarching makerspace project are described in the following "Methods and Results" sections. Because of the experimental direction in which we were taking this course, we agreed upon a mixed-methods approach for assessment, employing formative and summative and direct and indirect methods. These techniques included pre– and post–self-assessments (indirect summative), a project rubric (direct summative), team member evaluations (indirect formative), and two oral presentations with open Q&A (direct formative and summative). This section will focus primarily on data gathered from the pre– and post–self-assessment surveys. Preliminary analysis of the pre– and post–self-assessment survey results indicates that students gained competencies in both assembling effective teams and demonstrating their understanding of digital fabrication processes while completing the two homework assignments and the semester-long makerspace project.

These pre- and post-surveys were used to measure makerspace competencies for assembling effective teams. One problem with this type of tool is that it is unknown whether a student took the time to read and understand the survey questions and answer them fully and honestly. Some students probably clicked through quickly just to finish the survey. We used statistical analysis described by Horowitz and Golob[4] to assign each survey response an intra-class correlation coefficient based on comparison of students' pre- and post-survey responses. This process helped us identify and remove responses with a high probability of being unreliable, leaving twenty-two students in the study. All data and analysis provided herein is aggregated from those twenty-two students' participation in the study.

"Assembling Effective Teams" Homework Methods and Results

We adopted a similar technique using a survey developed in-house that was custom-tailored for the Assembling Effective Teams homework assignment. Our survey utilizes Likert-scale, multiple choice, and open-ended questions to collect data about students' experience with project management, team building, working in teams, digital fabrication, and other relevant PM topics.

The beta competency to assemble effective teams is comprised of five dimensions: "Recognizes opportunities to collaborate with others"; "Evaluates the costs and benefits of 'Doing-it-Together' (DIT) vs. 'Doing-it-Yourself' (DIY)"; "Seeks team members with skills appropriate for specific project requirements"; "Joins a team where his/her skills are sought and valued"; and "Solicits advice, knowledge and specific skills succinctly from experts." In order to measure the impact of the semester project on competency acquisition, we included questions about the first four of these dimensions directly into the survey tool. The questions asked students "How good are you with the following team building practices?" and listed the four dimensions. Answer options took the form of a Likert scale ranging from 1 to 5 (1 = *extremely bad,* 2 = *somewhat bad,* 3 = *neither good nor bad,* 4 = *somewhat good,* and 5 = *extremely good*). Students were able to use these four data points, combined with the project management data collected in the pre–self-evaluation survey, as criteria for creating their "Dream Team" and "Spread the Awesomeness" scenarios.

Additionally, we used Likert scales to capture knowledge about each type of fabrication technology that students were expected to learn and use while completing their semester project. The statement "Please rate your knowledge of how to use the types of equipment found at the UTA FabLab and other makerspaces" was followed by the list of equipment: 3D Printers, Laser Cutter/Engraver, CNC Vinyl Cutter, Screen Printing Press, Sewing Machines/Serger, CNC Embroidering Machine, CNC Mill/ShopBot, and File

Preparation for Digital Fabrication (Software). We used a 7-point Likert scale (1 = *none*, 2 = *beginner*, 3 = *novice*, 4 = *intermediate*, 5 = *competent*, 6 = *advanced*, and 7 = *expert*).

All the questions about digital fabrication processes and technology were included in the same survey used for the Assembling Effective Teams homework, and the responses were included in the data used by students to complete the Assembling Effective Teams homework assignment, adding to the "real-world" data that students were able to use to complete that assignment.

Students who assented to participate in this study answered these questions again at the end of the semester in a post–self-assessment survey. In the post–self-assessment survey, students were asked how good they were with the four team-building practices after having completed the project in the makerspace, and they were also asked to reflect back to the beginning of the semester and reevaluate how competent they were with team-building practices before completing the makerspace project. Combined, we collected three data points from each student on all four dimensions of the competency. We can compare these three values in aggregate to get an idea of how much students over- or underrated their competency when they answered the pre–self-assessment survey and to compare their competency ratings before and after completing the makerspace project. Figure 6.10 shows the aggregate averages for the three values.

FIGURE 6.10

Aggregate data for beta competency 4: Assembles Effective Teams

Dimension of competency	Average from pre-assessment	Average from post-assessment (reflection)	Average from post-assess-ment (now)
Recognizes opportunities to collaborate with others	3.18	3.18	3.64
Evaluates the costs and benefits of Doing-it-Together (DIT) vs. Doing-it-Yourself (DIY)	3.14	3.00	3.55
Seeks team members with skills appropriate for specific project requirements	3.41	3.27	3.73
Joins a team where his/her skills are sought and valued	3.18	3.14	3.73

Having the students design their own teams with a skill assessment data survey worked well. The assignment allowed them to create their own teams based on real-life data. For purposes of data analysis, we wanted students to reflect on how good they believed they were in the four dimensions of beta competency 4, "Assembles effective teams," during the post–self-assessment, so that the data would truly represent students' self-evaluation at the time of the post–self-assessment, rather than rely on the self-evaluation that they provided at the beginning of the semester. We predicted that students' self-evaluations at the beginning of the semester would be distorted either high or low because many of them had likely never encountered a situation requiring them to intentionally, methodically, and thoughtfully assemble a team based on real-world data and criteria such as found in the Assembling Effective Teams homework assignment. Therefore, it seemed likely that students would simply make their best guess about these dimensions of assembling teams. We used the two values for each dimension gathered in the post–self-assessment survey ("reflection" and "now," as shown in figure 6.10) to show students' actual improvement after having completed the makerspace project.

From the data, we can see that students tended to overestimate their competencies at the beginning of the semester by an average of 2.46 percent. This percentage is derived by averaging the percentage difference for all four dimensions in figure 6.10, "Average from pre-assessment" and "Average from post-assessment (reflection)." In the same fashion, we can see that across all four dimensions, students increased their competencies since the beginning of the semester by an average of 14.07 percent, derived by averaging the percentage difference for all four dimensions in figure 6.10, "Average from post-assessment (reflection)" and "Average from post-assessment (now)." Figure 6.11 shows the distilled data.

Digital Fabrication Homework Methods and Results

We used a similar pre– and post–self-assessment survey method for assessing beta competency 8, "Demonstrates understanding of digital fabrication process." Beta competency 8 includes three dimensions: "Recognizes additive and subtractive fabrication techniques," "Applies 3D modeling principles," and "Creates 3D models using appropriate software." Rather than using

FIGURE 6.11

Competency overestimations at pre-assessment for beta competency 4: "Assembles effective teams"

Dimension of competency	% Over-estimate at pre-assessment	Average difference	% Increase in competency (reflec-tion vs. now)	Average improvement
Recognizes opportunities to collaborate with others	0.00	0.00	12.64	0.46
Evaluates the costs and benefits of Doing-it-Together (DIT) vs. Doing-it-Yourself (DIY)	4.46	0.14	15.49	0.55
Seeks team members with skills appropriate for specific project requirements	4.11	0.14	12.33	0.46
Joins a team where his/her skills are sought and valued	1.26	0.04	15.82	0.59
Average	2.46		14.07	

Likert scales to measure these three dimensions, we employed open-ended essay questions to better capture technology, software, and process literacy for each. Survey items included the following: "Explain the difference between additive and subtractive fabrication techniques," "List the graphic design and 3D modeling software that you have used," and "Describe the 3D modeling principles that you might consider during the digital design and fabrication process."

Just as with the post–self-assessment for beta competency 4, students who assented to participate in this study answered both the open-ended essay questions and the Likert-scale technology questions again in a post–self-assessment survey at the end of the semester; again, students were asked to reflect back to the beginning of the semester and reevaluate their knowledge of makerspace equipment before completing the makerspace project. Figure 6.12 shows some examples of answers to the open-ended questions; the answers in each row are from the same student, but not all rows are from the same student. Figure 6.13 shows the aggregate averages for the three equipment knowledge values for each type of equipment.

FIGURE 6.12

Sample answers from the digital fabrication processes open-ended essay questions

Question	Answer from pre–self-assessment survey	Answer from post–self-assessment survey
Explain the difference between additive and subtractive fabrication techniques.	"Subtractive is where the 3d printer cut from a material to make the shape and additive is where 3d printer building the design where the materials are on a layer."	"Additive is start building up the object from the zero. example, 3d printing. Subtractive works the opposite way by cutting the object we want to form from a whole materiel. example, shop bot."
List the graphic design and 3D modeling software that you have used.	"catia, creo, solidworks, autocad LT"	"solidworks, creo, catia, aoutocad, for 3d design experience and inkscape for digital design"
Describe the 3D modeling principles that you might consider during the digital design and fabrication process.	"I would make sure not to make materials too thin, make each connection thorough with no accidental spaces, and make holes large enough for easy removal of the mesh filler."	"Designing for structure over looks"

FIGURE 6.13

Knowledge of FabLab equipment

Equipment	Average from pre-assessment	Average from post-assessment (reflection)	Average from post-assessment (now)
3D Printers	2.45	2.73	3.73
Laser Cutter/Engraver	1.55	1.81	2.45
CNC Vinyl Cutter	1.41	1.50	2.00
Screen Printing Press	1.23	1.36	2.23
Sewing Machines/Serger	2.27	2.09	2.64
CNC Embroidering Machine	1.50	1.45	2.27
CNC Mill/ShopBot	1.59	1.50	2.73
File Preparation for Digital Fabrication (Software)	2.00	2.27	3.59

We anticipated that after having completed the digital fabrication home-work assignment, and having completed their makerspace projects, students' essay answers would reflect a richer use of makerspace and digital fabrication jargon, a broader collection of software use, and more detailed descriptions of digital fabrication processes. The sample responses in figure 6.12 weigh up against our expectations in the following ways.

The sample answers in the first row of figure 6.12 show a slight improvement in the student's knowledge of subtractive fabrication. By the end of the semester, the student appears to have learned that a 3D printer does not cut into material and instead has listed the ShopBot as a subtractive fabrication technology. However, the student's general understanding of additive versus subtractive manufacturing didn't appear to change much. This is an example of a student appearing to maintain about the same degree of knowledge. This scenario is predictable for engineering seniors who have most likely had exposure to both additive and subtractive fabrication technologies at some point in their cohort.

The sample answers in the second row of figure 6.12 show a much more obvious increase in experience with digital fabrication software. Most of the software products listed in the post–self-assessment were present in the pre–self-assessment, but the student has added the software Inkscape for digital design, which presumably the student had not used prior to taking this course. This was a trend among students who answered the surveys—most had picked up experience with one or two new software products. Anec-dotally, during their final presentations, nearly every team acknowledged that its members had to use software that they had never used before, most notably VCarve, Illustrator, Photoshop, GIMP, and Inkscape. In this case, the oral presentations confirmed survey results, which lends to the validity of this survey question.

The sample answers in the third row of figure 6.12 are an example of the inverse of what we expected to see. The student clearly got lazy or impatient and didn't take the time to fully answer the question in the post–self-assess-ment survey. If the answers were taken seriously, we would have to draw the conclusion that the student left the course knowing less about 3D modeling principles than the individual started with. Sadly, this sample exemplifies the majority of the open-ended essay answers we received. We can imagine that at the end of the semester, students simply won't take the time to answer these types of questions, especially when the surveys are not graded and are completely voluntary. For the most part, students answered these questions fully and honestly in the pre–self-assessment survey, but that survey was part of the Assembling Effective Teams homework assignment, was required of all students, and was factored into the homework grade.

From the equipment knowledge Likert-scale data, we can see that for each of the technologies listed in figure 6.13, students tended to underestimate their competencies at the beginning of the semester by an average of 5.22 percent. This percentage is derived by averaging the percentage difference for all eight types of technology in figure 6.13, "Average from pre-assessment" and "Average from post-assessment (reflection)." In the same fashion, we can see that across all eight types of technology, students increased their knowledge from the beginning of the semester by an average of 31.97 percent, derived by averaging the percentage difference for all technology types in figure 6.13, "Average from post-assessment (reflection)" and "Average from post-assessment (now)." Figure 6.14 shows the distilled data.

FIGURE 6.14

Equipment knowledge underestimations at pre-assessment

Equipment	% Underestimate at pre-assessment	Average difference	% Increase in equipment knowledge (reflection vs. now)	Average improvement
3D Printers	11.43	0.28	26.81	1.00
Laser Cutter/ Engraver	16.77	0.26	26.12	0.64
CNC Vinyl Cutter	6.38	0.09	25.00	0.50
Screen Printing Press	10.57	0.13	39.01	0.87
Sewing Machines/Serger	-7.93	0.18	20.83	0.55
CNC Embroidering Machine	-3.33	0.05	36.12	0.82
CNC Mill/ ShopBot	-5.66	0.09	45.05	1.23
File Preparation for Digital Fabrication (Software)	13.50	0.27	36.77	1.32
Average	5.22		31.97	

SUMMARY

In general the integration of makerspace into the Engineering Project Management course was successful. The students enjoyed using the UTA FabLab according to their student evaluations, faculty nominated me for a teaching award for my work with the makerspace, and our Industry Advisory Board expressed interest in my work when I presented the project to them.

The Maker Literacies team will continue to work with this and other courses for makerspace-course integration and will continue collecting data about the competencies gained when completing projects in makerspaces. Because we are still in the early stages of this research, there is much room for improving our data collection and validation methods. As we improve our data collection and validation methods, we will also begin looking for patterns to emerge from the data and identify possible correlations between the different data points; for example, we may be able to answer questions about student perceptions of their competencies and how self-perception changes after exposure to working in makerspaces. Future work will also go more into depth on the other assessment methods used in the course (i.e., project rubric, peer evaluations, and oral presentations). We believe that analysis drawn from those sources may help support data gathered by the surveys and will show where these methods corroborate one another and where they show disparity.

NOTES

1. W. Edwards Deming, *The New Economics: For Industry, Government, Education,* 2nd ed. (Cambridge, MA: MIT Press, 1994).
2. J. J. Moder, C. R. Phillips, and E. W. Davis, *Project Management with CPM, PERT, and Precedence Diagramming,* 3rd ed. (New York, NY: Van Nostrand Reinhold, 1983).
3. H. Kerzner, *Project Management,* 12th ed. (Hoboken, NJ: John Wiley and Sons, 2017).
4. A. D. Horowitz and T. F. Golob, "Survey Data Reliability Effects on Results of Consumer Preference Analyses," *Advances in Consumer Research* 6, no. 1 (1979): 532–38.

Establishing an Ecosystem of Makers on Campus

Sarah Hutton

O pening its doors in September 2013, the Digital Media Lab (DML) in the W. E. B. Du Bois Library was originally constructed to provide multimedia production support for the undergraduate student population at the University of Massachusetts Amherst (UMass Amherst). Over the past six-plus years of operation, the space, services, staffing, and equipment have more than tripled, reflecting increasing demand not only for the support of multimedia production but also in response to emergent technology and curricular support across the campus. Though the DML is physically situated in the library, its growth stretches far beyond walls defined by departments, academic divisions, and geographic location. A vast ecosystem of support has developed across campus and throughout the community, which provides a foundation for how the UMass Amherst Libraries can engage with the maker community and makerspace curriculum today. Establishing a widespread, interconnected ecosystem requires a flexible growth strategy, a creative mindset, and deep roots; a strong anchor is essential to ground an idea as it germinates and spreads far beyond the original concept at its genesis. The most apt analogy for this type of augmentation and adaptability can be drawn from the natural world.

TARAXACUM OFFICINALE: AN ECOSYSTEM FRAMEWORK

In *Emergent Strategy,* adrienne maree brown introduces Janine Benyus's biomimicry as a way to think about organizational change strategy in the context of the natural world.[1] In biomimicry, you approach solving a challenge or problem by copying a process, form, or shape, looking to the ecosystem level for mimicking a solution. Complex Movements, a Detroit-based artist collective, draws this parallel between the natural world and community transformation. Each example from the natural world—mycelium, starlings, ferns, and so on—speaks to interconnected systems, where even the most minute changes can impact an entire organization, frequently without a central leader orchestrating direction. The Complex Movements' natural model presents the dandelion as representative of decentralization and resilience; the dandelion epitomizes an ecosystem that is incredibly difficult to uproot. Likening the development of the DML to that of the dandelion seems the most appropriate way to articulate a grassroots movement that has taken root and expanded beyond library walls.

GERMINATION: DEVELOPMENT OF THE DIGITAL MEDIA LAB AT UMASS AMHERST

Though definitions of *multimedia* may vary, it can be rudimentarily described as compositions of different forms of content and, in our particular context, predominantly digital. Many instructors have embraced multimedia and digital scholarship projects as a means for transitioning students from the traditional position of information consumerism to a role of producer, author, and scholar. In 2009 the University of Massachusetts Amherst Libraries began investigating the circulation of multimedia equipment to students, predictive of a changing curricular landscape in which learners would continually be encouraged to engage in creative multimedia scholarship. Preliminarily, we began with Vixia Camcorders to capture video, a few handheld and lavalier microphones, and home-grown portable audio recording booths; the intent was to be able to offer the "basics" for students conducting fieldwork. This initiative was piloted in the W. E. B. Du Bois Learning Commons, a centrally located place that brings together collections access, research support, and technologies focused predominantly on undergraduate student success. Following the implementation of this pilot, changes in course assignments began to increase, integrating more digital project assignments for students. Although our smaller pilot had proven very successful, there were no complementary spaces on campus that aimed to be accessible to the general student population.

As course requirements for students continued to change, support for student scholarship outside the classroom needed to change in tandem. In 2012 we recognized that we were reaching a critical point at which student support needs outside the classroom were no longer being met on our campus. Restricted access to equipment-rich multimedia production labs was frequently tied to funding provided via enrollment in specific programs, and, though film studies and communications students may have been able to gain access to the technology and support they needed, the general student population was at a loss. Trends in multimedia production across the curriculum prompted us to think of a new model of support. Interest in pursuing the development of space, services, and a collection of equipment was shared by stakeholders within the university Libraries, as well as throughout information technology, the faculty, and the student senate(s). Because of the interdisciplinary nature of a changing curriculum and our focus on broad access for all students, a campuswide group of stakeholders decided early on that centrally locating this new support model in the library was essential.

Assessing Campus Need

Needs assessment was collaboratively conducted across the campus, asking faculty, students, and support staff about their understanding of changes needs, which served us in establishing a gap analysis for preexisting support. Following multiple focus groups, case study analyses, and pulse surveys, a task force worked to build the Digital Media Lab in the W. E. B. Du Bois Library. This task force included membership from the Libraries, information technology (IT), faculty, and student populations to ensure broad representation for developing an inclusive operation for a broad audience. Preliminary planning focused on supporting burgeoning needs in general education courses, such as those in first-year writing, where digital storytelling was rapidly increasing as a project assignment, replacing the traditional research paper. We focused on digital making early on, aligning closely with learning outcomes articulated in humanities courses traditionally underserved by high-tech classroom and lab spaces. The positioning of the DML contributed greatly to a consistent focus on undergraduate education and curriculum mapping early on. Alongside the interdisciplinary, undergraduate-focused Learning Commons, the DML was established not within a library or IT department focused on supporting emerging technologies research but in one that focused specifically on the integration of library research literacies into the undergraduate curriculum. Situated in the Student Success and Engagement Department, the DML would work to align with the overarching departmental goals, articulated in a strategic planning document, to

> advocate for, promote, and provide innovative technologies, spaces, and education that will most effectively allow undergraduates at UMass and the Five Colleges to become creative, technologically adept, and critically engaged. Deliver personalized service in support of a user-centered organization to ensure the academic success of our students. Work to create equal access to and support of educational resources for citizens of the Commonwealth.

Staffing with a Focus on Curriculum Integration and Peer Leadership

A focus on undergraduate curriculum mapping in the nascency of the planning process would later lead to rapid adoption and high use of our proposed DML facilities, which initially included three main components: a green screen video recording room, an equipment circulation desk, and soundproof audio recording booths. Beyond facilities, our most pressing need to ensure student support was staffing. As an organization with a heavy focus on experiential student leadership opportunities, we began experimenting with peer-led workshops offered by students in fall 2012, prior to the lab opening in 2013. The staffing model for the workshops would serve as proof of concept for staffing the DML once it officially opened its doors for operation in 2013; a full-time lab coordinator position was filled in late 2012, and this individual guided the recruitment and hiring of additional full-time staff to oversee a predominantly student-led service model.

During the first year of operation, the DML collaborated with faculty and students to support courses spanning a broad range of disciplines, including comparative literature, anthropology, public health, and English. Digital storytelling, oral history projects, and podcasts proved to be the most frequently supported course assignments. Support of multimedia project work would start with entire class sections coming into the lab to receive workshop training on best practices in recording and digital project management, from storyboarding through the final editing process in production. These group workshops would be followed by the availability of open labs and expert support in the tools needed for project completion. During the early months of operation, we reviewed space usage and activity in the DML to adjust our hours of operation, moving our support to later in the day and evening, matching peak production activity. The wide variety of support across equipment, software, and tools encouraged high use of the space, and our interest in broadening our support offerings began within the first year of operation.

In early 2014 we began investigating the integration of 3D printing into our operations to provide an additional medium of creation for our students. We began by reviewing curriculum demands on the horizon, speaking with faculty partners who were conducting research in fabrication about resources they would need to support the integration of this type of research and production into their teaching portfolios. Our preliminary investigations were fast-tracked in late 2014 when an opportunity arose to partner with MakerBot to install a 3D Printing Innovation Center. In May 2015 we opened the first MakerBot 3D Printing Innovation Center to be installed in a university library.

TAKING ROOT: BRIDGING THE GAP BETWEEN THE DIGITAL AND PHYSICAL REALMS

Unlike the original project concept and initial development of the DML to support digital making, the necessity to develop a support plan for 3D printing and maker-based assignments required a much faster pace. The installation of the MakerBot 3D Printing Innovation Center brought forty-nine replicators, five digitizers, and three handheld object scanners into our inventory on a time line that did not provide the luxury of conducting a thorough campus needs assessment as we had intended. What this rapid time line *did* provide was the necessity to grow our network on campus, seeking out partnerships with other fabrication labs, courses in architecture, and the arts to establish proof of concept for a workable support model—*fast*.

In parallel with conversations regarding equipment and 3D printer networking requirements for installation, we conducted environmental scans on campus and beyond to investigate staffing models, policies, and protocols for supporting 3D printing. Talking with staff in well-established UMass Amherst labs such as M5, a makerspace space dedicated to supporting electrical engineering students, and the Advanced Digital Design and Fabrication (ADDFab) Lab, a space supporting state-of-the-art metal and polymer printing, we kickstarted our understanding of what would be necessary to take on this new direction. Many newcomers to 3D printing may not realize that this extension into the physical realm of fabrication requires deeper understanding of animation, electronics, engineering, and a slew of emerging technologies. In shifting a staffing model originally created to support student digital making and scholarship to one that would be supporting physical fabrication, we had to completely alter our approach.

Establishing a new full-time position for 3D printing oversight was definitely a catalyst for stretching our institution's understanding of the role of libraries and librarians; 3D printing, emerging technologies, and making are more frequently seen as falling squarely in the realm of engineering, physics, and architecture. In early 2015 research on makerspaces in public and community libraries was growing, but there was a limited understanding of how this shift in academic libraries could support academic success in higher education. Through building supportive networks and developing an ecosystem of partners from other departments and early adopters across campus, we were able to add the Libraries to the conversation. When the question "Why libraries?" would arise during the 3D printing discussion, multiple campus stakeholders were increasingly seeing the value of having fabrication and high-end technology resources and support centrally situated and *accessible* to all students.

Focusing on a student-led model of support in the DML had multiple benefits beyond our initially intended peer leadership and skill development opportunities for our student staff. Hiring student talent from across the campus in multiple disciplines provided the additional opportunity for faculty and research engagement. Acting as communicators to help grow our ecosystem throughout the university, these students talked with their friends and with their faculty about potential opportunities for new projects and development in collaboration with the DML. An early connection of note occurred with one of our founding 3D printing undergraduate students. Mechanical engineering major Kasey Smart connected his learning in the DML position with his work on the collaborative invention of the Beastcam[2] in the Biology Department's Irschick Lab. This new device, a camera and computer system that produces 3D images in seconds, is capable of capturing high-end scans of living objects. With regular, free access to professional-grade modeling software such as Autodesk Fusion 360, creative thought and application to research could be applied to this project outside regular lab hours; the Digital Media Lab, though not staffed twenty-four hours daily, provides access to all software and high-end processing iMacs twenty-four hours a day, five days a week. An early connection with the rapidly growing and now world-renowned Digital Life project provided the DML the opportunity to have conversations about where we could further develop our support, what our own technological limitations might be, and how we could best refer researchers seeking higher-end technology. This is an early example of growing that ecosystem beyond the borders of the library and helped launch conversations with other groups on campus interested in course collaborations and research partnerships.

Early Adoption and Proof of Concept: College of Education

The focus on interdisciplinarity and making resources accessible to all students in the DML allowed for experimentation and coursework spanning multiple subject areas beyond initial connections in the sciences. An early collaboration with courses and research in the College of Education forged a pathway for this work by providing proof of concept and examples we could share with multiple disciplines. Having previously connected on the digital making front with courses such as Educational Video Production and Designing Digital Media for Teaching and Learning, the DML was already recognized as a resource for support in emerging technologies, and taking the next step into 3D printing was a natural transition.

Following the receipt of a UMass Amherst College of Education Research Fellowship Grant, Drs. Torrey Trust and Robert Maloy collaborated with the DML on "3D Printing 4 Teaching and Learning," a study focused on developing a 3D printing, teaching, and learning community of practice for teachers. Recognizing the need to support learning opportunities for preservice and in-service K–12 educators, this study focused on the development of lesson plans integrating emerging technologies related to 3D printing and maker competencies. In alignment with the College of Education's focus on the transformation of student learning and teaching maker competencies to future educators, we were able to establish the groundwork for our commitment to deep integration of making into the curriculum early on and had the products from this work to showcase to other faculty who were considering the integration of making into their own courses. In addition to pointing faculty toward carefully reviewed and vetted resources on teaching 3D printing in higher education, we had several printed teaching models to share as examples (figure 7.1).

FIGURE 7.1

Collection of 3D printed project outputs from "3D Printing 4 Teaching and Learning" research, including dome structures

Outreach Strategies within Campus and Surrounding Communities

As we began establishing these initial course and research partnerships, we leveraged proof of concept by showcasing the physical output in the DML. The W. E. B. Du Bois Library has a long history of supporting site visits from groups interested in myriad topics ranging from our collections to the collaborative service model in the Learning Commons to the instructional support we can offer to many community organizations in our role as a public land-grant institution that serves the Commonwealth. Within the DML's home department, Student Success and Engagement, there is additionally a focus on connecting with campus residential programs, tours, new student orientations, and several other outreach programs dedicated to showcasing the resources that our campus has to offer to prospective and incoming students. Adding to an already full collection of resources the Libraries had to offer our patrons, DML staff expanded a tour of the space to bring additional focus to a display of 3D printed objects with prepared explanations of their origin and connection to course collaborations. A mobile showcase was also designed to travel and maintain a presence at library exhibit tables as a part of new student orientation, student activities fairs, and discipline-specific events such as the Information and Communication Technology (ICT) Summit.

The mobile showcase, in combination with promoting 3D printing through publications designed in collaboration with our library Development and Communications office, served to spread awareness of the accessibility to and support offered by the DML. Community organizations such as the 4-H Club and Girls Inc. as well as local schools began reaching out to receive orientations, tours, and hands-on programming experiences for students, faculty, and support staff. Our ecosystem continued to grow outside the university walls into the surrounding communities, spearheading conversations with local organizations in Amherst and sparking new conversations with local school districts in the Pioneer Valley. As awareness spread, our support grew to reflect increasing interest, and we modestly grew our staffing and resources to support this rapid growth in outreach support, programming, and equipment circulation. With this growth in our resources came the opportunity to deepen our course collaborations at the university.

RIPENING CYPSELAE: CURRICULUM INTEGRATION BRINGING FRUITS TO OUR LABORS

Considering how makerspaces impact student learning can frequently become an afterthought when focusing on the development of physical spaces and service models. With the introduction of an opportunity to explore the integration of maker-specific competencies into the undergraduate curriculum, we welcomed a potential research partnership with the University of Texas at Arlington (UTA) on the Maker Literacies grant. When UMass Amherst Libraries were initially approached in 2017 for potential partnership, we eagerly shared our ongoing developments with the team in the hopes that we could expand our burgeoning curriculum integration strategy. Prior to partnering on the Maker Literacies grant, we had only just begun to explore opportunities for course partnerships across campus.

Among several opportunities to integrate into interdisciplinary courses, the Commonwealth Honors College at UMass Amherst offers connection through partnership with experimental Honors Discovery Seminars. These one-credit seminars allow students to explore a specific topic in depth; topics are chosen by individual Honors instructors, and each section is open to students of any major, without advanced knowledge of the topic being necessary.

Honors faculty are drawn from multiple colleges throughout the campus, providing a broad swath of disciplines spanning the arts and humanities, STEM, and interdisciplinary collaborative topics. A few early adopters of 3D printing and maker curriculum began inquiring about resources the DML had to offer in support of their courses, given the focus of the lab on supporting students. As this reputation of the DML as an accessible fabrication hub spread, we were able to establish connections with one of these courses that would prove to offer deeper collaboration and focus on connecting the Libraries with maker competencies.

Honors Discovery Seminar: Adventures in 3D Printing

This initial Honors Discovery Seminar, Adventures in 3D Printing, was taught by Senior Lecturer and Building and Construction Technology (BCT) Coordinator Alex Schreyer. In addition to focusing on the development and printing of consumer goods, this course invited students to consider issues surrounding the ownership and copyright of ideas, as well as accessibility. Most important, though taught by an instructor in architectural design, this course offered opportunity for students from multiple subject areas to participate. Although Alex had resources to support the instruction of students in 3D printing, his interest was in how students would be able to complete their course projects outside class time, and the DML had the solution. This initial partnership brought these students into our lab space to receive equipment orientation and instructional support on design and fabrication, while also offering support and consultation for students when they needed to finalize designs and print their final course projects.

BCT 420: Designing with 3D CAD and BIM

Partnering with Alex Schreyer again as a part of the Maker Literacies grant research, we were able to deepen our exploration of connecting his Designing with 3D CAD and BIM (Building Information Modeling) course within the Building and Construction Technology program with more concrete student learning outcomes. Again facilitating selected class sessions in the DML to support software, design, and fabrication needs, we also worked with Alex to address two separate beta literacies in his course (see appendix A): applies design praxis; and demonstrates understanding of digital fabrication process. The products designed in this civil engineering course ranged from the artistic to the practical, all in alignment with these literacies that had been baked into the course syllabus.

The initial partnership with Alex sparked the interest of another faculty member in public policy and environmental conservation who was also interested in 3D printing but wanted to broaden the conversation into makerspaces, the maker culture, potentiality, and possibilities. Partnering on a course dedicated to 3D design and modeling is a natural fit; however, pairing with a course with a disciplinary focus as broad as the DML's could help us launch exploration into previously unexplored subjects.

SPP 597M: Makerspace Leadership and Outreach

SPP 597M, Makerspace Leadership and Outreach, is taught by Professor Charlie Schweik, who holds a joint appointment shared by the Department of Environmental Conservation and the Center for Public Policy and Administration. A long-time champion of open access and open educational resources, Charlie had intersected with the university Libraries on many occasions during his tenure, and a connection with this class was made early on to see how we could support continued development. The Makerspace Leadership and Outreach course shares many of the fundamental philosophical approaches espoused by the DML, emphasizing a focus on interdisciplinary dialogue, learning by doing, and creating an open culture of support and scholarship. In this course, students are invited to approach a topic or problem in local and global communities and seek out potential solutions, and collaborative support is provided to help them *build* that solution. The goal of the course is for students to use maker technologies and spaces to develop and demonstrate problem-solving capabilities in multiple environments and disciplines.

In addition to emphasizing public versus private goods and openly sharing research relying on open access and copyleft fundamentals, another unique characteristic of this course is the focus on fostering longitudinal research projects. By orienting to an open platform of knowledge sharing, projects selected and worked on by students could be passed on semester to semester, engaging other student groups as well as local and global researchers in the iterative research and design process. A local example of this model can be seen in an air quality sensor project, one which spanned research that started in 2014 in Environmental Health Science Professor Rick Peltier's Aerosol Lab and continued through an iterative research process into the fall of 2018. Originally designed to address asthma concerns by detecting air pollutants in Springfield, Massachusetts, this sensor is intended to be a low-cost device for local communities to gather readings on particulate matter, ozone, and carbon monoxide. Sharing this research and the device prototype openly, we were able to hand the project to students in the Makerspace Leadership and Outreach course to continue development, such as prototyping new 3D-printed encasements to reduce air turbulence that had been impacting data collection and investigating how to reduce the cost of production to make the device more accessible to under-resourced communities.

Another example of the benefit of this longitudinal, open research model is the development of a water sensor, which originated at the University of Los Andes (Uniandes) in Bogotá, Colombia. In the mining regions of the Amazon rainforest, there is widespread use of mercury to separate gold from soil particulates and sediments. This artisanal, small-scale gold mining is leaching dangerous levels of mercury into local water supplies, with the potential to poison mass populations. The idea was to start research and development on a low-cost water sensor that could be used by local villagers to test community river systems for heavy metals. Faculty at the University of Los Andes developed the first open-source version of a water sensor that measured temperature, dissolved oxygen, phosphorous, and conductivity in water.

In the fall 2017 Makerspace Leadership and Outreach course, a UMass Amherst student team sought to replicate the sensor built by the student team in Bogotá. Meeting online, students at Uniandes described their sensor to the UMass Amherst team; the Open Science Framework was used to share project documentation. Over two semesters, the UMass Amherst team developed a new version of the device, inserting an Arduino microcontroller into the original design. The project has now reached the point where controlled testing of the sensor is required; similar to the aforementioned air sensor project, UMass Amherst faculty again volunteered expertise and controlled testing environments in support. Faculty members at both universities are discussing a collaborative grant proposal to continue the project.

In fall 2017 we approached Professor Schweik to gauge his interest in participating in the Maker Literacies grant project; although we had previously been partnering with Schweik in support of his course, we had not yet brought instruction of this class into the DML. He agreed that this would be an interesting opportunity to explore the efficacy of this experiential learning course more deeply through the integration and measurement of an embedded set of maker literacies. By collaboratively teaching this course with Schweik in the DML, we were able to engage students in the conversation about open access and critical appraisal of their research process early on, introducing them to open research searching platforms and research impact strategy searching and making their scholarship openly accessible to a global audience. Also, because this course was facilitated by the library, students had an easier connection to our specialists in intellectual property and copyright, patent, and marketing research as well as subject-specific research. Over the course of a three-semester partnership, we continued to outfit our space to securely store projects under development with access provided to the students who wanted to continue their research and tinkering well after traditional lab hours; the W. E. B. Du Bois Library is open twenty-four hours a day five days a week, and we wanted to extend working opportunities to these students whenever their creativity was at its peak.

Exploring this collaboratively taught course through the Maker Literacies grant research provided the opportunity to report on how this course was successfully supporting student academic success with greater specificity. Students were already identifying the need to invent, design, fabricate, build, repurpose, or repair some "thing" in order to express an idea or emotion, or to solve a problem (competency 1 in appendix A); they were employing effective knowledge management practices (competency 5 in appendix A); and they were clearly transferring knowledge gained into workforce, community, and real-world situations (competency 11 in appendix A; these now map to competencies 1, 11, and 12 in the revised list of competencies in appendix B). However, by baking these literacies into the syllabus from the start, we were better equipped to communicate these outcomes not only to the students but to the campus community and other stakeholders. This capability to communicate impact on student success via concrete literacies allows us to translate this work more effectively and scale it to meet the needs of multiple groups and organizations.

PAPPI PARACHUTING: SCALING MAKER PRINCIPLES FOR SPREADING TO A GLOBAL COMMUNITY

In 2018 we were approached by UMass Amherst Summer Programs to offer a very broadly defined experiential research experience to a visiting group of students from the United Arab Emirates (UAE). The UAE Innovation Ambassadors Program was developed by the UAE Ministry of Education with the intent to instill modern educational approaches into various academic disciplines; by sending student delegates to sites in the United States, Switzerland, and the Netherlands identified as being on the forefront of innovative educational practices, the UAE can have these students then return to leadership roles at their home institutions and contribute to sustained educational change. We recognized immediate potential in connecting this group with the Makerspace Leadership and Outreach course and set to work scaling this semester-long class to a two-week accelerated research experience.

Sticking with the fundamentals of openness, longitudinal research, and addressing global environmental issues, we also kept in alignment with the intent to have students identify a problem, research potential solutions to that problem, and produce something that they could take back to their home institutions. An additional goal beyond making in this course for these particular students was to expose them to innovative educational models outside their more traditionally Socratic approach to learning in the UAE. In the initial pilot in 2018, we had students focus on identifying specific problems within more generalized areas of green technology, climate issues, and imported labor and articulated the main course outcome:

> The main goal of this seminar is to bring something back—a conceptualization of a project, which aims to solve a real-world problem; this solution could be anything from a solid fabricated object, to a recorded video or audio file, digital story, or compelling editorial piece. The intent is to engage your creative problem-solving skills and work within teams toward a shared solution.[3]

This acceleration of the Makerspace Leadership and Outreach course provided us the opportunity to draw from and appreciate the vast maker ecosystem we had established across the campus and into the community. Similar to how we start off our semester-long course, we began with an overview of makerspace principles and potentialities—the basics of DIY culture and open research, which are relatively new concepts to many of these students. In the first week, we exposed these students to as many lab and hands-on experiences as possible, ranging from visiting the high-end ADDFab Lab to participating in breadboard electronics workshops in the M5 Lab to a new experience for the 2019 cohort of helping to build out community maker workshop areas in LaunchSpace, a community makerspace in Orange, Massachusetts. This vast exposure to new ideas, spaces, places, and opportunities in that first week helped students think outside traditional approaches and start considering themselves makers (figure 7.2). Reflective student papers were integrated into that first week of the course, asking the

FIGURE 7.2

3D-printed bust scans of female students from the United Arab Emirates wearing hijabs. This image shows some members of the inaugural student cohort of the UAE Innovation Ambassadors Program in summer 2018. The DML is slated to continue its collaboration with the Ministry of Education for the third year in summer 2021; the program structure will remain anchored in the UN's Sustainable Development Goals (SDGs).

students specifically what their understanding of a makerspace is and if they consider themselves makers; comparing their perceptions at the beginning and end of this accelerated course shows a remarkable transition in thinking.

During the second week of the program, we drew from the experiences shared in site and lab visits, workshops, and programming offered in the DML covering fundamentals in 3D printing, video production, and augmented and virtual reality (AR/VR) and helped the students shape their research into solutions. Having also provided instructional sessions on scholarly research, open access, and copyright, we supported the development of their research along the way to foster an understanding of what it means to be "open" in scholarship and why it is so important. The outcomes of that scholarship were presented to the campus community: In 2018 students gave digital presentations, which for some groups included the demonstration of a product prototype. In 2019 the students presented their research in a more formal poster session, which required the additional integration of a poster design workshop focusing on how to best communicate research and the importance of findings to an intended audience. The outcomes of the first year of programming in 2018 were incredibly impressive, ranging from pool sensors that help reduce high levels of child drownings in the UAE to Arduino noise sensors that help open-concept office and research spaces self-monitor ambient noise levels to the repurposing of farm waste into a sustainable energy solution. Some groups were more focused on developing a physical product prototype, while others were focused on policy development and communicating the urgency of their problem to their home communities. The incredible progress made during such a short time was quite astounding; we are currently working toward how to best share this scholarship with the global community and plan to continue our partnership with this summer program.

CONCLUSION: APPRECIATION FOR THE TAPROOT

When it comes to makerspaces in higher education, we are often scrambling to highlight better, faster, stronger, more *visible* solutions to support a community of makers. In campus tours and recruitment materials, makerspaces are often highlighted as an attractant to prospective students for all the beneficial reasons we can cite in our instructional work and research on maker literacies relating to interdisciplinary collaboration and "collision space," experiential learning opportunities, and design thinking. However, this focus on building "the ultimate space" and having all the cutting-edge materials in one centralized location may be a concept that is inaccessible to many institutions seeking to foster a culture of making on their campus. Although providing the appropriate equipment is certainly important, the heart of the maker culture should be the development of what is a good fit for your institution—that is, a culture of openness, creativity, and connection. Libraries have a longstanding history of fostering community, openness, and connection that cuts across every discipline. By making these connections and building an ecosystem of support, you can provide incredible learning opportunities for your students that stretch far beyond library walls into the global community. The Maker Literacies developed through this collaborative research endeavor allow for scalable, measurable exploration of new partnerships and development opportunities worldwide.

NOTES

1. Adrienne M. Brown, *Emergent Strategy: Shaping Change, Changing Worlds* (Chico, CA: AK Press, 2017).

2. "Undergrads Help Invent 'Beastcam,'" University of Massachusetts Amherst, https://www.umass.edu/giving/undergrads-help-invent-%E2%80%9Cbeastcam%E2%80%9D.

3. C. Schweik and S. Acquah, LLSR and 011-SEC01 Innovation Ambassador Program course syllabus (Amherst: University of Massachusetts Amherst, 2019).

Faculty Collaborations to Put Maker Competencies into Course Assignments

Anna Engelke, Bryant L. Hutson, Kelly A. Hogan,
Joe M. Williams, Danianne Mizzy, Megan Plenge, Jennifer Coble,
Josh Corbat, and Mark McCombs

n this chapter, we describe how faculty teaching four different undergraduate-level courses at the University of North Carolina at Chapel Hill (UNC-Chapel Hill) applied the beta maker competencies (see appendix A) to support student learning through maker projects. As part of this effort, these faculty participated in faculty learning communities (FLCs) related to making; collaborated with librarians and with makerspace and assessment staff; and engaged in self-reflection in order to more effectively implement the competencies. Using formative and summative evaluation data, including course syllabi, assignment descriptions, rubrics, faculty feedback surveys, faculty follow-up interviews, and student learning outcomes, we will report on both the successes and challenges of the maker competencies implementation process. We also offer discussion and implications for other higher education educators interested in supporting faculty in integrating the competencies into maker projects to promote student learning.

PROJECT CONTEXT

The Be A Maker (BeAM) network of makerspaces at UNC-Chapel Hill offers any UNC student, staff member, or faculty member the opportunity to design and create physical objects for education, research, entrepreneurship, and recreation. The materials, tools, consultations, and trainings are all provided at no cost to the user. Thus, unlike on many campuses where making is confined to discipline-specific programs such as art or engineering, there is a budding culture of making for everyone on our campus. The program currently serves more than four thousand users per year from disciplines across the arts and sciences, as well as professional schools such as education, public health, and medicine.

UNC Libraries was a founding member of the campus maker education initiative. Through participation in the 2015 IMLS-funded Making + Learning convening, UNC librarians were introduced to the Making + Learning project framework and brought those ideas back to campus. In 2015 they began to design educational experiences that were grounded in constructivist learning theory and that focused on a host of student learning outcomes beyond tool mastery.

In 2017 the campus initiated a large-scale accreditation project called the Quality Enhancement Plan (QEP) that intentionally incorporated design thinking and making into undergraduate courses to support experiential, hands-on learning. Making was incorporated into the QEP because a large infrastructure to support making (i.e., numerous maker spaces) was already prevalent on campus for several years before the QEP was initiated. Making was not tucked away in an engineering department. Rather, a culture was in place that promoted making as something everyone could do. Nonetheless, the majority of maker projects were extracurricular in nature, often produced to give as gifts. Only a fraction of these projects had a student practicing design and iteration because many were simple replicas. The QEP was an opportunity to experiment with curriculum and infuse making with disciplinary learning, whether that be in the sciences or arts and humanities.

The QEP courses and the courses involved in this Maker Literacies project were being developed in tandem. In fact, the two helped inform each other. For example, several of the staff involved worked closely with both projects. The maker education specialist, a BeAM staff member, was working to train faculty in both the QEP and the Maker Literacies project in collaboration with Kenan Science Library (KSL) staff. There were two faculty members in common, as well as the same QEP assessment director. BeAM staff, KSL staff, and the QEP assessment director held joint consultations with faculty, facilitated course development workshops, and worked together to support faculty while they prototyped their maker projects. Both the QEP and the Maker Literacies project were developed through an iterative process that allowed them to inform each other. For example, the beta maker competencies (appendix A) were used to inform the revision of introductory QEP workshops for the 2017–2018 Makerspace Faculty Learning Community, as well as revisions to the surveys used in maker courses that are part of the QEP. The QEP has also provided insights that frame our recommendations for how others can approach the adoption of the maker competencies, found in the "Discussion and Implications" section later in this chapter.

Four faculty members and one doctoral student were involved in this Maker Literacies project, and each had different prior experiences with maker projects. The geology and biology instructors had integrated maker projects in their courses previously, whereas the math and education instructors and the doctoral student did not have experience with maker projects in their courses. None of the instructors were familiar with the eleven University of Texas at Arlington (UTA) beta maker competencies prior to this project (see appendix A).

FACULTY REACTIONS TO THE MAKER COMPETENCIES

Faculty responses indicated general alignment between the maker competencies and faculty members' own prior experience with design thinking. For example, one faculty member responding to a feedback survey focused on personal experience with design thinking relative to curriculum design: "Many of the competencies align with those of curriculum design, particularly in the real-world contexts of schools where time and materials are always in a limited supply." Additionally, the geology professor immediately noticed that many of the competencies aligned with what she was already doing in the class. These competencies included identifying the need to design and build "things," analyzing and exploring questions, and producing prototypes, along with other competencies geared toward collaboration and the application of knowledge. The education doctoral student found a similar alignment:

These competencies integrate very well into a course on Education. In particular, I can see focusing on the following as highly beneficial to pre-service teachers developing a critical conception of teaching and learning: "employs effective knowledge management practices" and "identifies the need to invent, design, fabricate, build, repurpose or repair some 'thing' in order to express an idea or emotion, or to solve a problem."

INCORPORATING MAKER COMPETENCIES INTO COURSES WITHOUT EXISTING MAKING ASSIGNMENTS

The mathematics and education faculty members, who were exploring maker projects for the first time, were introduced to the competencies through individual consulting sessions with the BeAM maker education specialist, the KSL librarian, and the QEP assessment director on campus. Using the student learning outcomes identified for their specific courses, these faculty members identified discipline-based assignments that utilized the making process to facilitate student learning. Then they engaged in an iterative process to identify corresponding competencies as they developed a novel assignment rubric to be shared with their students (figure 8.1).

The education course provides one example of this developmental and iterative process. In this course about children's literature, the maker project required preservice teachers to make a postmodern, nonlinear book to be used with children. Initial consultation discussions about the book assignment led the instructor to elaborate on an assignment rubric that she could use to measure discipline-based learning outcomes. As the assignment description became more concrete, the instructor and the education specialist selected specific making competencies. The instructor then revisited the assignment description and how the assignment contributed to the overall course objectives.

The math instructor found that the competencies greatly informed the way he first designed the assignment, in which students explored the intersection of art and mathematics through the creation of modular origami structures. Beta competency 2, "Applies design praxis"—and especially the dimension related to revising and modifying prototype design over multiple iterations—was particularly informative and led the math instructor

FIGURE 8.1

Beta maker competencies, learning outcomes, rubric criteria, and assignments

	Planet Earth Lab, GEOL 101L with Lab (n = 275)	Math, Art, and the Human Experience, MATH 58 (n = 24)	Principles and Methods of Teaching Biology, BIOL 410 (n = 12)	Children's Literature in Elementary and Middle Schools, EDUC 567 (n = 40)
Competencies	1, 2, 3, 4, 5, 6, 7, 11	1, 2, 3, 4, 5, 6, 7, 11	1, 2, 3, 4, 5, 6, 7, 11	1, 2, 3, 4, 5, 6, 7, 11
Learning Outcomes	Apply the scientific method, including the formulation of scientific questions and the use of multiple working hypotheses, to solve problems concerning Earth processes.	Illustrate that they can analyze the problem and break it into component parts; acquire reliable and relevant background information for the project; identify and work effectively within project constraints; take intelligence risks and learn from failures; seek assistance when needed from team members/classmates who have skills that fulfill specific project requirements; assist team members/classmates when his/her skills are sought and valued; seek advice, knowledge, and specific skills from experts when needed.	Illustrate the central, unifying concepts of biology; design hands-on manipulatives and/or models and accompanying curricula to support deeper understanding of biology among high school students; integrate appropriate technology to enhance instruction in science; design learning experiences that make the central concepts of biology accessible, meaningful, and culturally relevant for diverse learners; design developmentally appropriate strategies to deliver instruction in science; apply best practice in science education and participate in the dissemination of those ideas; foster relationships with practicing science teachers; provide outreach, service, and leadership to the science education community.	Explore literature in the contexts of interdisciplinary elementary and middle school curricula and the interests and needs of children and young adolescents.

(cont.)

FIGURE 8.1 *(cont.)*

Beta maker competencies, learning outcomes, rubric criteria, and assignments

	Planet Earth Lab, GEOL 101L with Lab (n = 275)	Math, Art, and the Human Experience, MATH 58 (n = 24)	Principles and Methods of Teaching Biology, BIOL 410 (n = 12)	Children's Literature in Elementary and Middle Schools, EDUC 567 (n = 40)
Rubric Criteria	Artifact (model); experimental results; maker competencies; class presentation	Artifact (accuracy and aesthetics); maker competencies—design praxis; maker competencies—effective teams	Content standards; maker competencies; student efforts; organization and presentation	Artifact (content and maker competencies); portfolio (process, organization, and collaboration); reflection
Assignments/ Artifacts	Develop a scientific research question; formulate an experiment; design a physical, numerical, or computer model; perform the experiment; analyze the results.	Cut design templates and construct a twenty-unit modular origami icosahedron sculpture in small groups; work individually to design and cut a template to create a curved-crease origami sculpture.	Model illustrating essential science ideas of selected abstract biochemical or cellular topics; accompanying curriculum including lesson plans and student worksheets; sharing through existing network of practicing teachers.	Create a post-modern text using maker technologies in small groups; create author statements and advertising materials; present final book and complete reflection.

to embed opportunities for iteration into his assignments. Students had to interpret physical paper templates in order to design line drawings in Adobe Illustrator with precise dimensions. These drawings would then support their fabrication on the makerspace laser cutter. Students sent their design files to the instructor, who sent the files back with screenshots annotated with suggestions. This process allowed students to iterate their design files toward a more reliable version that they could then send to the laser cutter, leading them toward further iteration within the fabrication process.

The faculty who created new maker assignments also received support from librarians and makerspace staff in designing, developing, and prototyping the projects they intended to complete with their students. Librarians, BeAM staff, and the QEP assessment director initially met as a team with faculty to help incorporate the Maker Literacies and identify ways to measure their impact on student learning. Thereafter, consultations took place individually or jointly, as needed. This practice-oriented process helped build empathy for the student experience, identified project milestones that corresponded to key competencies, and assisted in the refinement of the competency-informed assessment rubrics that were created. The process also supported the iteration of the course project and the rubrics, both of which were informed by and a practical application of the maker competencies.

For example, the math professor identified beta competency 6, "Assesses the availability of tools," and beta competency 7, "Assesses the availability of materials," as being key to the practice of designing and fabricating modular origami. He wanted his students to investigate the level of exactness required for various forms of cutting and folding. He proposed contrasting the precision of the makerspace's laser cutter with that of techniques done by hand. However, to fully determine how to best use this activity to serve the corresponding competency, he spent several weeks prototyping different origami structures on the makerspace laser cutter to compare its accuracy to that of traditional folding and scoring methods.

INCORPORATING MAKER COMPETENCIES INTO COURSES WITH EXISTING MAKING ASSIGNMENTS

The faculty members who were more experienced with the makerspaces were relatively confident about their existing making assignments and accompanying rubrics. The introduction of the eleven beta maker competencies, however, provided them with useful support as they refined their assignments and rubrics.

In the geology course, the making assignment required students to test hypotheses regarding geoscientific processes. Beta competency 4, "Assembles effective teams," prompted this instructor to revise the course project to include more opportunities for peer review and evaluation of team members. Through the project time line, students were required to look at each other's assignments, reflect on areas for improvement, and deliver this feedback in an effective manner. Students also received feedback on their projects from their teaching assistants (TAs) through structured, consistent, and collaborative meetings. Students reported that oral check-ins with their TAs helped them build confidence in their projects, as well as helping them move forward when they hit roadblocks.

In the biology course, the assignment centered on designing and fabricating manipulatives like puzzles, games, or models that can be used by high school biology teachers. The instructor's assignment rubric primarily focused on science concepts and science communication. Instead of incorporating the maker competencies explicitly into the rubrics, she used the competencies to frame the practices students used to fulfill the biology-based criteria. For example, she drew heavily from beta competency 2, "Applies design praxis," particularly the dimension "Takes intelligent risks and learns from failures." She wanted her students to persist through failure in their projects as a way of better understanding the challenges they might face as future science educators.

CHALLENGES WITH COMPETENCIES AND INCORPORATING MAKING

Some of the challenges expressed by faculty were focused on the beta maker competencies. For example, the geology professor expressed that the beta competencies were centered on learning the design process, but her goal was to use the design process as a way of learning the geology-based content. She had to continually balance how much time to spend on learning "best practices" of design and making with how much time to devote to building foundational knowledge in geological concepts that could inform the design. In this course, designing and making were used as tools for understanding course content, rather than as areas of study themselves. Therefore, TAs opted to spend time scaffolding student understanding of geoscience content rather than maker competencies, and many students opted to make their models out of materials that were familiar to them (e.g., modeling clay) rather than using the materials and equipment available to them in the makerspace.

The math professor found that integrating beta competency 4, "Assembles effective teams," was a challenge. Several students voiced strong reservations about working in groups, citing past negative experiences. Because of this concern, those students were allowed to work individually, despite the goal of having the projects be a collaborative experience. As a result of the challenge, the instructor intends to make the group work mandatory in future iterations of the course. He also wants to make the collaborative aspect of the project stronger to frame its value more clearly for the students. He plans to make those competencies related to teamwork and collaboration more clearly stated as part of the learning objectives, project, and assessment rubrics.

Several faculty members required students to complete maker projects in groups because these projects required a substantial time expenditure, both by the students completing the project and the instructor grading them. Complaints about group work were not limited to students in the math course; challenges in splitting up work fairly and finding meeting times outside class were often cited as reasons students wished to avoid group work. The geology professor handled this challenge by implementing two surveys, one at the midpoint of the project and one at the end of the project. In these surveys, students could anonymously rate the efforts and contributions of their teammates. Survey results were then converted into a numerical factor that could be applied to the total project score, alleviating the concerns of students whose groups had unfair work distributions. Faculty who plan to incorporate making into large courses may need support to determine how best to evaluate group work for such a complex project.

Depending on the disciplinary areas, some faculty commented on the challenge to integrate specific terms used in the competencies in their instructional settings (e.g., "critical paths" in beta competency 3 and "version control" in beta competency 5). One suggestion for improvement was to broaden the language to make it less technical, thus allowing the competencies to be more applicable across multiple disciplines. Given this feedback, revised language and expanded dimensions for these competencies can now be found in revised competencies 8 and 11, respectively (see appendix B, specifically the explanation provided in the "Avoiding Jargon in the List of Maker Competencies" section).

Other challenges reflected the difficulties of integrating making into a course. For example, the math professor recognized that students weren't always good at self-evaluating their work and were confused about how to visualize the criteria in the assignment rubric. They perceived that they had followed instructions and fulfilled the rubric criteria, when in fact they had not. In future iterations of the course, the instructor wants to use formative assessment with his students by having them use their final project rubric to informally grade their practice projects. He predicts that by using the final rubric for informal assessment throughout the semester, students will be able to identify a "successful" project versus one that "needs improvement."

The biology professor found it challenging to evaluate students on their design and making process. She felt confident in perceiving and evaluating student success throughout the semester based on her own experience and knowledge from previous semesters. However, she found it difficult to quantify certain characteristics of project work into a codified assessment tool. For example, when students struggled with setbacks during their projects, the professor wanted to recognize those students who approached challenges with resilience and persevered through challenges to advance their work. However, it was difficult to parse when a project stalled because of genuine limitations of the making process or because of a lack of motivation on the students' part to identify alternative solutions.

A significant challenge for the geology professor was rooted in the diversity of her students. Both geology majors and non-major students often took the same course sections together. She found that non-major students and younger students were often at a disadvantage, having to learn fundamental geological concepts as well as how to create effective experimental models at the same time. Collaborative work alleviated some of these concerns; however, she would like to find a more effective way to scaffold the project in the future, so that everyone can complete sophisticated projects. She is considering more tightly defining the specific geological content areas the students explore to give them a clearer place to start with their projects.

Faculty also reported challenges for students related to learning about new software, technology, and tools, especially for beginners who may not be familiar with these resources.

BENEFITS OF COMPETENCIES AND INCORPORATING MAKING

Some of the benefits that faculty reported centered on being able to more clearly see the learning occurring in their classes as it related to specific competencies. For example, beta competency 1 stated, "Identifies the need to invent, design, fabricate, build, repurpose or repair some 'thing' in order to express an idea or emotion, or to solve a problem." The biology professor found that the maker project revealed misconceptions that wouldn't have been discovered through writing a paper. Students found it challenging to simplify and portray real-world science through a model because teaching the concepts to others required a deeper conceptual understanding.

In this same course, students were assessed weekly through updates conducted during the ten weeks in which they engaged in the making process. As the instructor reflected on the process, she commented on beta competency 2 regarding utilizing iterative design principles:

> Viewing [students'] evolving model designs was most effective for me as this allowed me to assess their understanding of the biology concepts they were depicting in their models, their ability to identify the most essential concepts within their topic, which were the goal of their models and their Maker Literacy competencies by their evolving iterations.

The education doctoral student observed,

> Too often in undergraduate education courses, the focus is solely on teaching and learning, and we forget that the methods and materials used in the course have a profound impact on student learning and teacher development. By having the competencies to guide me, I can more fully integrate making into the broader course discussions.

While the faculty could directly measure learning through their assignment rubrics, the students were also asked to report their own growth in terms of making skills and confidence in making (see the "Discussion and Implications" section later in this chapter).

The benefits of learning were not limited to the assigned maker competencies. Faculty also reported discipline-based learning through the maker projects, which was also part of their assignment rubrics. For example, responding to a faculty feedback survey, the education professor reported on a writing reflection prompt related to students' experimentation with new materials and tools. She commented, "This is generally successful because it gives them a low-stress way to think deeply about their own learning."

A survey of students from the geology professor's courses showed that this project helped students gain both knowledge of scientific methodologies and confidence in their abilities to develop and test hypotheses. In addition, some of the students learned new skills or found new opportunities based on their experiences. For example, one of the students (a non-major) has been asked to construct a class set of earthquake shaker tables based on the design he created for the project.

Other benefits for student outcomes related to student emotions: responding to the feedback survey, one faculty member commented, "The students LOVED being able to make a physical product. They also gained a great deal of resilience from feeling the anxiety of not knowing how to do something, figuring it out and reflecting on their journey."

There were also numerous faculty benefits. On the feedback survey, the math professor commented, "My work on this project has inspired me to apply for an internal course development grant in order to completely redesign the Math/Art Seminar as a maker-based exploration [in] mathematics." Graduate student teaching assistants in the geology course found mentoring students through the design process to be particularly beneficial, and several said that their own understanding of the scientific process changed as a result of mentoring students through their experimental design and maker projects.

DISCUSSION AND IMPLICATIONS

Just as the making process is iterative, so is the development of a maker course and the associated assignments. All faculty mentioned this aspect in their reflections, whether they were new to making or more experienced. As a result, we found that all the faculty involved in this project found the beta maker competencies valuable, wherever those faculty were in their own developmental process. Many beta competencies were found valuable by all faculty (beta competencies 1, 2, 3, 4, 5, 6, 7, 11), although the dimensions within these competencies had varied usefulness. Some of the usefulness may hinge on the balance between teaching design-thinking and teaching discipline-specific concepts. Other competencies would be more useful if they were adjusted, such as by adding collaboration to more of the competencies, as suggested by one of the faculty members in this project.

We propose that the maker competencies can create a framework for supporting faculty in integrating design and making into their coursework. By doing so, faculty can envision how to use the competencies in their classroom by practicing them during their course development. The following discussion refers to the competencies by the numbering system used in the beta list (see appendix A); however, all these competencies, with slight revisions to the wording, still exist in the 2018 revised version (see appendix B).

As faculty begin the process of integrating design and making, we recommend that they start with beta competency 1, "Identify the need to . . . design . . . a new derivative of some 'thing' in order to express an idea or emotion, or to solve a problem." This competency maps directly to the process of redesigning a course to incorporate a maker project. We recommend consulting with an education specialist to work through understanding the meaning of the maker competencies and faculty members' own discipline-based learning goals, which could be framed with the dimension, "Recognize unmet needs that may be filled by making." Similarly, the beta competency 4 dimension, "Solicits advice, knowledge and specific skills succinctly from experts," can be addressed through conversations with faculty experienced in maker course integration.

Beta competency 2, "Applies design praxis," can frame the process of using clearly defined learning goals to determine appropriate design and maker projects. We recommend that faculty see the competencies as a starting place for their thinking, rather than focusing on all of them initially. Particularly helpful is the dimension, "Brainstorms for a variety of solutions and chooses the best one." Many times, it is helpful to think of a variety of projects that students could design and make and then step back to see which one matches most closely with the defined learning goals. Some categories of objects that may be helpful for faculty to brainstorm about include "tools of the trade" for their discipline, learning tools designed by students to teach specific concepts, or narrative objects that tell a story about some aspect of the content they are investigating.

After faculty identify one or two potential projects that are aligned to specific learning objectives, we highly recommend prototyping the assignments to refine them for clarity, scope, and feasibility. This process maps to several beta competencies, including beta competencies 6 and 7, related to assessing the availability and appropriateness of tools and materials, and

FIGURE 8.2
....

Interview questions for end-of-semester faculty reflection

Competency-Based Assignment Rubric Development

- How did you develop and revise the assignment and rubric based on your understanding of the maker competencies?
- Once the specific maker competencies were identified, did that help you go back and revise the assignment description or rubric or both? If so, can you give an example?
- In your opinion, which competencies might be challenging to integrate in the course you teach? Why?

Rubric Use to Support Student Learning

- How did you use the assignment rubric in your teaching?
- How did the use of competencies and assignment rubrics impact your instruction?
- How did the use of the competencies and assignment rubrics impact student learning?
- What do you think were the benefits of using the competencies and assignment rubrics in your class?
- What are some challenges to using the competencies and assignment rubrics?
- What changes have you made or do you plan to make to the project and assignment rubric since last implementation?
- What are some major lessons learned?

---

beta competency 2, especially the dimension related to creating and testing prototypes. By creating an example output from their assignment, instructors can evaluate the project's effectiveness in achieving the learning objectives, determine the resources and materials needed to support their students in the design and making processes, and identify key milestones of the project in order to hold students accountable throughout the course. This process also develops technical skills that faculty members can use to advise their students as they work on their projects.

We recommend that faculty recognize that their assignment rubrics, based on the competencies and discipline-based outcomes, will be iterative as they move through each successive semester (though standardized rubrics for each competency will be an outcome of future Maker Literacies grant work). This aspect can be framed with the beta competency 2 dimension that describes revising prototypes over multiple iterations as faculty participate in the design process alongside their students. As students are designing and making as part of their project, faculty are iterating their course design as part of their own creative undertaking. This process is also tied to beta competency 3, for which faculty will need to use the dimension "Outlines project milestones and identifies dependencies" for their students, but they will also need to remain flexible given the iterative nature of integrating design and making into coursework (i.e., "Builds in extra time to allow for multiple prototype iterations").

For any faculty member involved in making, the iterative process of effective course development requires reflection.[1] Many faculty members inherently do not build in time for reflection. Thus, we recommend that maker education specialists and library staff provide surveys that hold faculty accountable for reflection. As part of this project, faculty were asked through an end-of-semester survey about their experiences. However, the feedback from this survey felt somewhat lacking, so we also incorporated interviews with three of the four faculty members. We recommend that support specialists adapt the questions provided in figure 8.2 to help faculty better reflect on their course, the maker competencies, and student learning.

This project was run in parallel with the QEP project at UNC-Chapel Hill, in which faculty incorporating making were part of a yearlong faculty learning community (FLC). Because of the success of these FLCs, we would recommend this approach as a best practice for faculty engaging with maker projects and the maker competencies. The incorporation of an FLC is supported with framing from beta competency 4, especially the dimension "Recognizes opportunities to collaborate with others," where the value of peer collaboration within maker course integration can be clearly identified for new faculty. Ideally, an FLC would comprise faculty who are new to making and those more experienced, so faculty can learn from each other.

Faculty who participated in the maker FLC found that the meetings provided them with the time and space to reflect on the structure of their maker assignments, as well as brainstorm new ideas and practice evaluating maker projects. Many of the ideas discussed were emergent, with some of the most valuable focused on troubleshooting common issues, such as the formation of groups and the timing for iterative steps in the making process. These learning communities may also be avenues for professional development workshops highlighting both making-specific pedagogy (e.g., how to teach the design process, technical tool skills) and related but broader strategies for course design (e.g., developing learning objectives, utilizing group evaluations and overall assessment of an iterative project).

One critical factor in UNC-Chapel Hill's success was the team-based approach to providing faculty support in the areas of pedagogy, fabrication, and assessment. Our team-based approach was successful in large part because of the support our project received at the university level. That broad, organizational endorsement helped encourage collaborations across several departments and units and enabled staff availability for working on the project. Some of the formalized faculty support that we believe would be most beneficial for other institutions moving into this area includes in-depth consultations with librarians, makerspace staff, and assessment staff; FLC and professional development opportunities for making-specific and making-adjacent (e.g., evaluation, group work concerns) skills; and skill-oriented workshops related to makerspace course integration (e.g., developing learning objectives, maker assessment, technical tool skills).

The integration of the beta maker competencies into coursework at UNC-Chapel Hill was an iterative process. Faculty used the competencies to inform their course development and teaching, which saved them time in their planning, brought more clarity to assignments for students, and helped them see student learning more clearly. Their reflections informed our recommendations for best practices—namely, that professional development for faculty is critical for effectively using the competencies to support students. Faculty should be empowered to practice the competencies themselves through prototyping their projects, receiving peer feedback on their work, and continually reflecting on their experiences. This iterative development of a maker project leverages the design and making processes to encourage deeper thinking and engagement with course content.

NOTE

1. Patti Clayton and Sarah Ash, "Reflection as a Key Component in Faculty Development," *On the Horizon* 13, no. 3 (2005): 161–69, https://doi.org/10.1108/10748120510618187; Nishamali Jayatilleke and Anne Mackie, "Reflection as Part of Continuous Professional Development for Public Health Professionals: A Literature Review," *Journal of Public Health* 35, no. 2 (June 2013): 308–12, https://doi.org/10.1093/pubmed/fds083.

APPENDIX A
Beta List of Maker Competencies

The "Maker-Literate" student:

1. identifies the need to invent, design, fabricate, build, repurpose or repair some "thing" in order to express an idea or emotion, or to solve a problem
   a. recognizes unmet needs that may be filled by making
   b. expresses curiosity about how things are made and how they work
   c. "hacks" and "tinkers" to learn how things are made and how they work
   d. evaluates the costs and benefits of making as an alternative to buying or hiring

2. applies design praxis
   a. defines the problem
   b. analyzes the problem and breaks it into component parts
   c. acquires reliable and relevant background information
   d. identifies stakeholders
   e. specifies project requirements
   f. identifies and works effectively within project constraints, be they financial, temporal, proximal, or material
   g. brainstorms for a variety of solutions and chooses the best one
   h. evaluates the costs and benefits of using off-the-shelf parts or kits as opposed to making from scratch
   i. creates and tests prototypes
   j. revises and modifies prototype design over multiple iterations
   k. takes intelligent risks and learns from failures

3. demonstrates time management best-practices
   a. outlines project milestones and identifies dependencies
   b. constructs critical paths
   c. builds in extra time to allow for multiple prototype iterations

4. assembles effective teams
    a. recognizes opportunities to collaborate with others
    b. evaluates the costs and benefits of "Doing-it-Together" (DIT) vs. "Do-ing-it-Yourself" (DIY)
    c. seeks team members with skills appropriate for specific project require-ments
    d. joins a team where his/her skills are sought and valued
    e. solicits advice, knowledge, and specific skills succinctly from experts

5. employs effective knowledge management practices
    a. communicates clearly with team members and stakeholders
    b. restates technical and "maker" jargon in plain English
    c. documents work clearly
    d. uses version control to manage project outputs and documentation
    e. preserves project outputs and documentation for long-term access

6. assesses the availability of tools
    a. selects the best tools for the job
    b. acquires the necessary tools or revises project to conform to tool avail-ability
    c. seeks alternate tools when a required tool is not available
    d. creates necessary tools that can't be acquired or when an alternate is not an option

7. assesses the availability of materials
    a. selects the best materials for the job
    b. acquires the necessary materials or revises project to conform to mate-rials availability
    c. seeks alternate materials when a required material is not available

8. demonstrates understanding of digital fabrication process
    a. recognizes additive and subtractive fabrication techniques
    b. applies 3D modeling principles
    c. creates 3D models using appropriate software

9. understands many of the ethical, legal, and socioeconomic issues surrounding making
    a. demonstrates an understanding of intellectual property rights and protections
    b. identifies project outputs that may be protectable by trade secret, patent, trademark, or copyright
    c. compares the costs and benefits of seeking intellectual property protections vs. making project outputs open and freely available to others
    d. evaluates the costs and benefits of open-source and proprietary systems
    e. recognizes and respects the intellectual property rights of other makers

10. employs safety precautions
    a. seeks training for dangerous equipment and materials
    b. wears personal protective gear when appropriate
    c. teaches safety precautions to others

11. transfers knowledge gained into workforce, community, and real-world situations
    a. teaches what he/she knows to less experienced makers

APPENDIX B
Maker Competencies
(Revised December 2018)

HOW TO USE THE LIST OF MAKER COMPETENCIES

The list of maker competencies was developed specifically as a lesson-planning aid for faculty of undergraduate courses seeking to integrate academic library maker-spaces into their curriculum. For sure, the list can be used more broadly than this context. The competencies can apply to any semi-structured, formal, or informal learning environment in which learners apply hands-on problem solving in a creative studio-style space and in which teachers wish to gauge the development of competencies in their students.

The list was modeled largely on the *Information Literacy Competency Standards for Higher Education* (2000) promulgated by the Association for College and Research Libraries (ACRL) and can be used in much the same way. The ACRL standards opened the door for hundreds, if not thousands, of curriculum-embedded information literacy programs across the nation's universities. Due to the far-reaching success of the ACRL standards, and because the developers of the Maker Literacies program—for which this list forms the foundation—have experience with the ACRL standards and are now seeking to embed academic library makerspaces into the curriculum, the ACRL model was the ideal model to borrow from.

Items in the competencies list are designed to be mapped to existing or adopted as new student learning outcomes (SLOs) in courses that emphasize the types of trans-ferable skills exemplified by the list. The items should be used just like any other SLOs in the curriculum-planning process. This process usually begins with brainstorming a list of skills and concepts that an instructor expects students to learn by taking a specific course. This list is then narrowed to a set of realistically achievable outcomes, and the list of maker competencies is consulted to see if any items in the list correspond to the instructor's desired SLOs. In some cases, a broad category itself may be suitable as an SLO (categories are numbered 1–15 in the list); in other cases, it may be best to select one or more of a category's dimensions as SLOs (dimensions are indented beneath each category and labeled with lowercase letters). The list of competencies is not static and can be flexibly adapted to the instructor's needs.

Once maker competencies have been mapped to corresponding SLO counterparts, the next step is to design curriculum with the SLOs in mind. Assignments should include components that require students to use the makerspace while also reinforcing the SLOs. In the case of the Maker Literacies program, these components usually materialize as projects (individual or team-based) that require students to create an object in the makerspace, but often the assignment may take a different angle than making an object, or the object might not be something physically tangible, as most of current making suggests. Such items can be software for makerspace operations management, in the case of a computer science course, or a technical manual, in the case of an English course. In short, the term *making* should be interpreted broadly. While designing assignments, it is imperative that instructors consult with makerspace staff. Instructors should inquire about the types of equipment available in the makerspace and about the makerspace's staff and space capacity for providing services to the class. Knowing the benefits *and* limitations of the makerspace will help the instructor develop specifications for the assignment.

The last step is to develop assessment tools for measuring SLOs. These tools often take the form of analytical rubrics in combination with oral or written reflections from students. In short, assessment tools need to be designed to capture student competence gained by completing the assignment. In many situations, it may benefit the instructor to develop assessment tools before designing the assignment itself; this method is called *backward design* and is very common in competencies-based and online education, in which assessment takes center stage and assignments are carefully designed to ensure that assessment can be appropriately conducted. Whether one is employing traditional or backward design, the three steps described here are the essentials for good lesson planning, with well-crafted SLOs at the center of it all.

The Maker Literacies program website (https://library.uta.edu/makerliteracies) includes sample lesson plans from many faculty who have participated in the program. The lesson plans are released with Creative Commons licenses so that others may use them. As the Maker Literacies program continues to grow, so will the archive of lesson plans.

AVOIDING JARGON IN THE LIST OF MAKER COMPETENCIES

As with any domain-specific technical document such as this, jargon is almost unavoidable. The Maker Literacies Program Team has taken great care to eliminate extraneous jargon and to clarify unavoidable jargon by placing it within ample context for readers to gain understanding of its meaning.

Feedback from the program's beta-testing phase revealed the following four terms to be problematic jargon: *critical path, hack, tinker,* and *version control.* Critical path, originally a dimension of the beta-phase Time Management category, has been expanded as its own competency in the revised list: "Develop a project plan." The term *critical path* does not appear anywhere in the list, but the "Develop a project plan" competency, along with its dimensions, is an extrapolation of the meaning of *critical path.*

The terms *hack* and *tinker* remain in the list. For the purposes of this document, both these terms refer to the informal, exploratory acts of physical inquiry that students pursue in order to better understand a process or object. *Hacking* refers to the act of deconstructing an object to figure out how it works, then rebuilding it, often tweaking its original design for a new purpose. *Tinkering* refers to the trial-and-error process of making something out of serendipitously available parts and materials, without a plan, simply for the sake of learning how different things can be combined.

Last, the term version control has been expounded upon in the context of the "Employ effective knowledge management practices" competency. Version control is any system or method for keeping track of the various versions or iterations of a product or document.

LIST OF MAKER COMPETENCIES

Competencies
Makers will:

Ideate
1. Identify the need to invent, design, fabricate, build, repurpose, repair, or create a new derivative of some "thing" in order to express an idea or emotion, to solve a problem, and/or teach a concept
   a. recognize unmet needs that may be filled by making
   b. tinker and hack to learn how things are made and how they work
   c. evaluate the costs and benefits of making as an alternative to buying or hiring
   d. investigate how others have approached similar situations

2. Analyze the idea, question, and/or problem
   a. define the idea, question, and/or problem

    b. break the idea, question, and/or problem into its constituent parts

    c. question assumptions

3. Explore the idea, question, and/or problem and potential solutions
    a. garner input from stakeholders and peers
    b. research existing relevant products and ideas
    c. brainstorm a variety of solutions and pursue the most promising one
    d. evaluate the costs and benefits of using off-the-shelf parts or kits as opposed to making from scratch

Create

4. Operate safely
    a. seek training and information on dangerous equipment and materials
    b. ascertain applicable technical standards and safety codes
    c. wear personal protective gear when appropriate
    d. reinforce safety precautions with others
    e. accustom self with location-specific emergency procedures, egress and disaster plans
    f. observe safety procedures in the event a person(s) is impaired or injured
    g. transfer safety principles gleaned in training to broader contexts

5. Assess the availability and appropriateness of tools and materials
    a. research various equipment and materials to determine limitations and suitability for a specific application
    b. choose the most appropriate tools and materials (physical, digital, and rhetorical) for the job
    c. acquire the necessary tools and materials
    d. investigate alternate tools and materials when a desired tool or material is not available
    e. fabricate necessary tools, reimagine material choices, develop alternate workflows, and/or revise project scope when alternative tools or materials are not available

6. Produce prototypes
    a. determine the method of creation most suited to the project
    b. gain confidence with technologies and processes required for creation
    c. specify functional requirements for prototype vs. desired finished product

    d. divide design into individual components to facilitate testing

    e. document design process

7. Utilize iterative design principles
    a. apply measurable criteria to determine whether creation meets needs
    b. revise and modify prototype design over multiple iterations
    c. gather prototype feedback and input from stakeholders and mentors
    d. rework design to include insights from feedback
    e. take intelligent risks, use trial and error, and learn from failures

Manage

8. Develop a project plan
    a. identify who the relevant stakeholders are
    b. specify actionable and measurable project goals and requirements
    c. utilize time management and project management tools
    d. outline project milestones, including sequential action items
    e. anticipate time for multiple prototype iterations
    f. work effectively within project constraints, be they financial, material, spatial, and/or temporal

9. Assemble effective teams
    a. recognize opportunities to collaborate with others who provide diverse experiences and perspectives
    b. gauge the costs and benefits of "Doing-it-Yourself" (DIY) or "Doing-it-Together" (DIT)
    c. recruit team members with diverse skills appropriate for specific project requirements
    d. join a team where one's skills are sought and valued
    e. solicit advice, knowledge, and specific skills from experts

10. Collaborate effectively with team members and stakeholders
    a. listen to others
    b. learn from and with others
    c. communicate respectfully and clearly with team members and stakeholders
    d. follow through on team commitments and responsibilities
    e. practice accountability both personally and with team members
    f. appraise contributions to the success of the team

11. Employ effective knowledge management practices
    a. restate technical and maker jargon for the layperson
    b. document steps clearly with sufficient detail for others to follow and replicate workflows
    c. use version control to manage project outputs and documentation
    d. preserve project outputs and documentation for long-term access

Share

12. Apply knowledge gained into other disciplines, workforce, and community
    a. teach skills and share insights with other makers
    b. recognize and cultivate transferable skills
    c. transfer knowledge, skills, and methods of inquiry across disciplines and activities
    d. familiarize self with skill sets of others
    e. connect those seeking to learn something with those who have relevant experience

13. Be mindful of the spectrum of cultural, economic, environmental, and social issues surrounding making
    a. express awareness of diversity and inclusion when identifying unmet needs
    b. consider sustainability when making, including upcycling and recycling materials
    c. scrutinize the ethical implications of making

14. Understand many of the legal issues surrounding making
    a. demonstrate an understanding of intellectual property rights and protections
    b. weigh the costs and benefits of seeking intellectual property protections vs. making project outputs open and freely available to others
    c. examine the potential viability of both proprietary and open-source systems to adopt/adapt
    d. respect the intellectual property rights of other makers

15. Pursue entrepreneurial opportunities
    a. perform thorough market research for competing products and capacity for monetization

b. identify project outputs that may be protectable by trade secret, patent, trademark, or copyright

c. project costs of mass production and requisite economies of scale for return on investment

d. refine financial plan for variable scenarios

Dispositions and Values

Makers:

- Construct knowledge and understanding through doing.
- Reflect on what they have learned by making.
- Convey curiosity about how things work, how things are made, why they have been made that way, and how they might be improved.
- Celebrate opportunities to share skills, knowledge, ideas, and creations to benefit a broader community.
- Practice persistence through the problem-solving and iterative design process.
- Engage enthusiastically in opportunities to learn.
- Exhibit appropriate confidence in their ability to ideate, create, and problem solve.
- Embrace risk and innovation.
- Value collaboration and diverse perspectives and experiences.
- Appreciate openness and sharing.
- Comprehend that the objects one makes are tangible forms of embodied knowledge.

PROJECT PARTICIPANTS

This project was made possible in part by the Institute of Museum and Library Services (IMLS) National Leadership Grants for Libraries, LG-97-17-0010-17. IMLS is the primary source of federal support for the nation's libraries and museums. IMLS advances, supports, and empowers America's museums, libraries, and related organizations through grant-making, research, and policy development. The vision of IMLS is a nation where museums and libraries work together to transform the lives of individuals and communities. To learn more, visit www.imls.gov. The views, findings, conclusions, or recommendations expressed in this publication do not necessarily represent those of the Institute of Museum and Library Services.

The University of Texas at Arlington Libraries also acknowledges and extends its gratitude to all the library staff, makerspace staff, and faculty members who helped make this work possible, including but not limited to the following contributors to the beta and revised lists of maker competencies.

UTA Libraries Maker Literacies Task Force (March 2016–August 2017)

Amanda Alexander (Art Education)
Estee Beck (English)
Bonnie Boardman (Engineering)
Morgan Chivers (UTA Libraries, FabLab)
Katie Musick Peery (UTA Libraries, FabLab)
Kathryn Pole (Education)
Jennifer Roye (Nursing)
David Sparks (Science)
Gretchen Trkay (UTA Libraries)
Martin Wallace (UTA Libraries)

IMLS Grant Team (January 2017–December 2018)

Morgan Chivers (UTA)
Katie Musick Peery (UTA)
Tara Radniecki (UNR)
Gretchen Trkay (UTA)
Martin K. Wallace (UTA)

IMLS Grant Partner Site Coordinators (October 2017–June 2018)

Sarah Hutton (UMass Amherst)
Danianne Mizzy (UNC-Chapel Hill)
Tara Radniecki (UNR)
Amy Vecchione (BSU)
Martin Wallace (UTA)

Faculty Beta Testers (September 2016–May 2018)

Boise State University

Stephen Crowley (Philosophy)
Leslie Madsen-Brooks (History)

University of Massachusetts Amherst
   Alex Schreyer (Engineering)
   Charlie Schweik (Public Administration)

University of Nevada, Reno
   Nicole Miller (Fine Arts)
   Paula Noble (Geology)

University of North Carolina at Chapel Hill
   Jennifer Coble (Biology Education)
   Josh Corbat (Education)
   Jocelyn Glazier (Education)
   Mark McCombs (Mathematics)

University of Texas at Arlington
   Amanda Alexander (Art Education)
   Estee Beck (English)
   Kathryne Beebe (History)
   Bonnie Boardman (Engineering)
   Jaime Cantu (Engineering)
   Scott Cook (Fine Arts)
   Christoph Csallner (Computer Science)
   Christopher Kribs (Mathematics Education)
   Cedrick May (English)
   David Sparks (Science Education)
   Christian Worlow (English)

BIBLIOGRAPHY

American Library Association. "Access to Library Resources and Services." http://www.ala.org/advocacy/intfreedom/access.

American Library Association. "Core Values of Librarianship." http://www.ala.org/advocacy/intfreedom/corevalues.

Bicknell-Holmes, Tracy. "Why a MakerLab in a Library?" Boise State University. https://library.boisestate.edu/wp-content/uploads/2017/06/Why-a-Maker Lab-in-a-Library.pdf.

Blikstein, Paulo, S. L. Martinez, and H. A. Pang. *Meaningful Making: Projects and Inspirations for Fab Labs and Makerspaces.* Torrance, CA: Constructing Modern Knowledge Press, 2016.

Brown, Adrienne M. *Emergent Strategy: Shaping Change, Changing Worlds.* Chico, CA: AK Press, 2017.

"Campus Ethnic Diversity: National Universities." *U.S. News and World Report* (2019). https://www.usnews.com/best-colleges/rankings/national -universities/campus-ethnic-diversity.

Clayton, Patti, and Sarah Ash. "Reflection as a Key Component in Faculty Development." *On the Horizon* 13, no. 3 (2005): 161–69. https://doi.org/10.1108/10748120510618187.

"DeLaMare Science and Engineering Library First in Nation to Offer 3D Printing Campuswide." *Nevada Today,* July 19, 2012. https://www.unr.edu/nevada -today/news/2012/3d-copier.

Jayatilleke, Nishamali, and Anne Mackie. "Reflection as Part of Continuous Professional Development for Public Health Professionals: A Literature Review." *Journal of Public Health* 35, no. 2 (June 2013): 308–12. https://doi.org/10.1093/pubmed/fds083.

Kim, Youngmoo E., K. Edouard, K. Alderfer, and B. K. Smith. *Making Culture: A National Study of Education Makerspaces.* Drexel University, ExCITe Center, 2018. https://drexel.edu/excite/engagement/learning-innovation/making -culture-report.

Koh, Kyungwon, and June Abbas. "Competencies for Information Professionals in Learning Labs and Makerspaces." *Journal of Education for Library and Information Science* 56, no. 2 (2015): 114–29. doi:10.12783/issn.2328-2967/56/2/3.

Kolb, David A. *Experiential Learning: Experience as the Source of Learning and Development.* Englewood Cliffs, NJ: Prentice-Hall, 1984.

Kruger, Justin, and David Dunning. "Unskilled and Unaware of It: How Difficulties in Recognizing One's Own Incompetence Lead to Inflated Self-Assessments." *Journal of Personality and Social Psychology* 77, no. 6 (1999): 1121–34.

Kuglitsch, Rebecca. "Teaching for Transfer: Reconciling the Framework with Disciplinary Information Literacy." *portal: Libraries and the Academy* 15, no. 3 (July 2015): 457–70.

Lachapelle, Richard. "Experiential Learning and Discipline-Based Art Education." *Visual Arts Research* 23, no. 2 (1997): 135–44.

Lankes, R. David. "Killing Librarianship." Keynote speech at New England Library Association, Burlington, VT, October 2, 2011. https://davidlankes.org/rdlankes/Presentations/2011/KillLib.htm.

Mathews, Brian. "Think Like a Startup: A White Paper to Inspire Library Entrepreneurialism." 2012. https://vtechworks.lib.vt.edu/handle/10919/18649.

McNamee, Gregory. "Erasing the Gap between Art and Science." *Science Magazine—Careers,* May 2001. https://www.sciencemag.org/careers/2001/05/erasing-gap-between-art-and-science.

Musick Peery, Katie, and Morgan Chivers. "Diversity by Design: How to Create and Sustain an Inclusive Academic Library Makerspace." In *Re-Making the Library Makerspace: Critical Theories, Reflections, and Practices,* edited by Maggie Melo and Jennifer Nichols. Sacramento, CA: Library Juice Press, forthcoming.

Musick Peery, Katie, and Morgan Chivers. "Intentionally Cultivating Diverse Community for Radically Open Access Makerspaces." White paper presented at the International Symposium on Academic Makerspaces, Stanford, CA, 2018. http://hdl.handle.net/10106/27574.

Roberts, Jay W. *Experiential Education in the College Context: What It Is, How It Works, and Why It Matters.* New York, NY: Routledge, 2016.

"Undergrads Help Invent 'Beastcam.'" University of Massachusetts Amherst. https://www.umass.edu/giving/undergrads-help-invent-%E2%80%9Cbeastcam%E2%80%9D.

White, Sonia L. J., L. Graham, and S. Blass. "Why Do We Know So Little about the Factors Associated with Gifted Underachievement? A Systematic Literature Review." *Educational Research Review* 24 (2018): 55–66.

ABOUT THE CONTRIBUTORS

REBECCA BICHEL has been an academic librarian for more than twenty years and is currently dean of libraries at the University of Texas at Arlington (UTA). She received her BS in economics and BBA in business economics in 1991 from Valdosta State University and her MLIS in 1995 from the University of Hawaii. She joined UTA in 2012 after roles at Florida State University, Pennsylvania State University, and Sam Houston State University. Rebecca's areas of expertise are organizational change and innovation in libraries. Under Rebecca's leadership, UTA Libraries has developed student-centered spaces and programs for experiential learning, including the UTA FabLab.

JAIME CANTU is an assistant professor of industrial manufacturing and systems engineering at the University of Texas at Arlington. He received his PhD in systems and engineering management from Texas Tech University. His research incorporates economic decision analysis, organizational performance measurements, and system modeling. His work with high reliability, resilience, and modeling/measuring complex organizations has led to modeling urban farmer/food bank logistics in the Dallas-Fort Worth area and measuring integration of makerspaces into coursework.

MORGAN CHIVERS graduated from San Jose State University (2011) with four simultaneously conferred degrees: BA in history, BA in global studies, BFA in photography, and BFA in spatial arts (minors: anthropology, music, religious studies, German, environmental studies). Morgan earned an MFA in glass/intermedia (2015) at the University of Texas at Arlington (UTA), where he is now the FabLab librarian and artist-in-residence, collaborating with faculty to integrate making and digital fabrication into curriculum across a beautifully diverse campus. As an author, Morgan has published about his studio practice, pedagogy, and the innovative work of the UTA FabLab, regularly presenting at conferences nationally and internationally.

JENNIFER COBLE is a teaching associate professor at the University of North Carolina at Chapel Hill. A former high school science teacher, Jennifer now teaches science teaching methods and internship courses that allow science majors to get their high school teaching license while they earn their degree. In 2014 she integrated making into her methods courses so the preservice teachers could make physical models of science phenomena, which will be assembled into curriculum kits and shared with high school science teachers.

JOSH CORBAT is a teacher and early career education researcher with a focus on qualitative methods of exploring innovative teaching and learning. As a high school science teacher, Josh had a strong interest in exploring cutting-edge technologies and pedagogies in his classroom, a passion he now brings into his work with preservice and in-service teachers.

ANNA ENGELKE is the education program manager for the BeAM network of makerspaces at the University of North Carolina at Chapel Hill (UNC-Chapel Hill). Her work focuses on educational projects, primarily oriented toward supporting faculty with integrating design, making, and the BeAM makerspaces into their course curriculum. Previously, she served as the program manager for tinkering and technology at the Museum of Life and Science in Durham, North Carolina. She earned her master's degree in education technology, innovation, and entrepreneurship from UNC-Chapel Hill in 2017.

KELLY A. HOGAN is a teaching professor of biology and associate dean of instructional innovation at the University of North Carolina at Chapel Hill. Her research and administrative work have focused on inclusive and innovative teaching methods in higher education, including course-based undergraduate research experiences and makerspace courses. She has written several publications and an upcoming book about inclusive pedagogy and is also the author of several biology textbooks.

BRYANT L. HUTSON is the director of assessment for the University of North Carolina at Chapel Hill. His research focuses on faculty development, academic advising, and the use of assessment in higher education.

SARAH HUTTON is the head of Student Success and Engagement at the W. E. B. Du Bois Library, University of Massachusetts Amherst (UMass Amherst). Her research is focused on the intersection of student motivation theory, creative/alternative scholarship, and open educational resources. She is a librarian, artist, and PhD candidate in educational policy and leadership at the UMass Amherst College of Education.

MARK MCCOMBS is a teaching professor of mathematics at the University of North Carolina at Chapel Hill, where he earned his BS, MS, and MAT degrees. He teaches the first-year seminar Mathematical Origami and Fractal Symmetry, a maker-based course designed to cultivate students' analytical creativity. He has received the Students' Undergraduate Teaching Award, the Learning Disabilities Access Award for Teaching, the Institute for Arts and Humanities Chapman Faculty Fellowship, the Tanner Award for Excellence in Teaching, and the Goodman Petersen Award for Excellence in Teaching Mathematics. He enjoys designing and creating 3D origami sculpture and digital fractal art; one of his sculptures is now on display in Stockholm's National Museum of Science and Technology.

DANIANNE MIZZY is currently associate university librarian at Cornell University. At the University of North Carolina at Chapel Hill (UNC-Chapel Hill), she helped launch the Kenan Science Library Makerspace and the campuswide Be A Maker@Carolina makerspace network. She served on the Quality Enhancement Plan implementation committee that established a making program for all UNC undergraduates. She was the principal investigator for the IMLS/LSTA-funded Triangle Learning Network planning grant.

MEGAN PLENGE is a teaching assistant professor in the geological sciences department at the University of North Carolina at Chapel Hill. She teaches earth science courses that incorporate nature of science concepts, including how observational data can be used in conjunction models to inform us about phenomena that cannot directly be observed. Her research focuses on how students' confidence, attitudes, and interest in geoscience relate to teaching methodology.

TARA RADNIECKI is the head of the DeLaMare Science and Engineering Library at the University of Nevada, Reno. Her work and research focus on the impact of makerspaces and other emerging technologies within higher education library settings. Her interests also extend to intellectual property, and she has authored numerous publications on both topics.

GRETCHEN TRKAY is the department head for Experiential Learning and Outreach at the University of Texas at Arlington Libraries. Her work and research center on teaching transferable skills through course-integrated, project-based learning and engaging students in creative enterprise and exploration through experiential learning programming. She is involved in several grant-funded projects intended to result in tools and professional development focused on the integration of making into K–12 and undergraduate curricula.

AMY VECCHIONE is an associate professor and unit head of emerging technologies and experiential learning at Albertsons Library at Boise State University. Her research focuses on accessibility for all to use emerging technologies. She has published on accessibility, emerging technologies, and identity and making. She is currently coauthoring a book on how library staff can collaborate for student success.

MARTIN K. WALLACE is an experiential learning librarian and liaison to engineering, math, and physics at the University of Texas at Arlington (UTA) Libraries. He specializes in intellectual property, information literacy, experiential learning, and assessment. In his previous role as Maker Literacies librarian, Martin led UTA Libraries' effort to develop maker-based competencies and assess student learning in the UTA FabLab (UTA's academic library makerspace).

JOE M. WILLIAMS is the director of public services for the University Libraries at the University of North Carolina at Chapel Hill (UNC-Chapel Hill). Since earning his MSLS from UNC in 2001, his career and professional interests have focused on change management, service design and assessment, learning spaces, and the integration of new tools and technologies in teaching and learning.

INDEX

McCombs, Mark
  as faculty beta tester, 155
  "Faculty Collaborations to Put Maker
    Competencies into Course Assignments,"
    127–142
  information about, 161
*Meaningful Making: Projects and Inspirations for
  Fab Labs and Makerspaces* (Blikstein, Martinez,
  & Pang), 56–57
milestones, 95
Miller, Nicole, 155
Mini Mav (semester project)
  description of, 92
  final podium design, 96
  final product, 98–99
  final stable design, 96
  proposed podium design, 95
  proposed stable concept, 94
  requirements for, 92–93
Mizzy, Danianne
  "Faculty Collaborations to Put Maker
    Competencies into Course Assignments,"
    127–142
  as IMLS grant partner site coordinator, 154
  information about, 161
MLTF
  See Maker Literacies Task Force
mobile showcase, 117
multimedia, 110–111, 113
Multiple Teaching Practices in Mathematics and
  Science (Education 4333) course, 28
Musick Peery, Katie
  on grant writing team, 25
  Maker Literacies program, beginning of,
    69
  on Maker Literacies Task Force, 22, 154
  preface, vii–ix

N

National Association of Colleges and Employers
  (NACE) Job Outlook 2016, 23
National Science Foundation, 19
natural world, 110
needs assessment, 111–112
Noble, Paul, 155
noise, 37

O

Object-Oriented Software Engineering
  (Computer Science and Engineering 3311)
  course, 28
open platform, 120–121
open scholarship, 124
open-ended questions, 104–105, 106–107
openness, 125
origami fabrication assignment, 130, 133
outreach
  by Digital Media Lab, 117
  Makerspace Leadership and Outreach,
    120–122

P

PBL (project-based learning), 29
PCB milling machine, 38
peer leadership
  Digital Media Lab staffing with focus on,
    112–113
  peer-led workshops at DML, 111–112
Peltier, Rick, 120
PERT (Program Evaluation and Review
  Technique) analysis, 97
Planet Earth Lab (GEOL 101L with Lab)
  benefits of competencies/making in
    courses, 138
  beta maker competencies, learning
    outcomes, rubric criteria, assignments,
    131–132
  challenges of incorporating competencies
    into, 134, 135
  making assignment for, 133–134
planning, 90
play, 5–6
Plenge, Megan, 127–142, 161
PM certificates, 88
PMI (Project Management Institute), 88
PMP (Project Management Professional), 88
Pole, Kathryn
  on grant writing team, 25
  on Maker Literacies Task Force, 22, 154
pre- and post-surveys, 102–107
prebooked consultations, 46
Principles and Methods of Teaching Biology
  (BIOL 410)
  benefits of competencies/making, 137

CPSIA information can be obtained
at www.ICGtesting.com
Printed in the USA
LVHW010901110821
694572LV00005B/13